ENGLISH SHOP-FRONTS

OLD AND NEW

ENGLISH SHOP-FRONTS

OLD AND NEW

A SERIES OF EXAMPLES BY LEADING ARCHITECTS · SELECTED AND SPECIALLY PHOTOGRAPHED · TOGETHER WITH DESCRIPTIVE NOTES AND ILLUSTRATIONS

BY

HORACE DAN, M.S.A.

AND

E. C. MORGAN WILLMOTT, A.R.I.B.A.

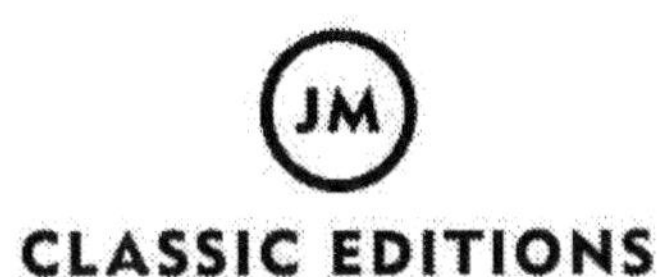

This edition digitally re-mastered and
published by JM Classic Editions © 2007

ISBN 978-1-905217-74-8

PREFACE.

NO apology is needed for the publication of a volume upon shop-fronts, a subject full of architectural interest. Owing to a mistaken policy of economy on the part of shop-keepers, or a feeling that an unbroken display of glass was all that was necessary, the erection of the shop-front has usually been left more or less to chance, with a result quite disastrous from an architectural point of view. A reaction has, however, set in, and many leading architects have of recent years given attention to the design of this important feature of street architecture.

It is hoped that the undoubted merit of a large number of the carefully selected examples given in this book will persuade architects in general that the shop-front has infinite possibilities of good architectural treatment. It may also help commercial men to understand the qualities that make an artistic and effective front. It is desirable that the shop-keeper should realize that with a general public gradually becoming more appreciative of what is not commonplace or vulgar in design, it behoves him to make his shop-front architecturally interesting and attractive.

To Mr. Dan has fallen the task of seeking for and photographing most of the examples, Mr. Willmott having undertaken the writing of the descriptive notes, and the preparation of the illustrations to Chapter III.

The proprietors of "The Architectural Review" were

good enough to place the illustration of No. 137, Long Acre, London, at the disposal of the publisher, while to Mr. George Walton the authors have to tender their thanks for the loan of the illustration of the Kodak Shop, Brussels, and the working drawings of No. 40, West Strand. Mr. C. G. Harper has kindly allowed the publisher to reproduce his effective drawing of the old Bulk Shop in Clare Market. The illustration of the old shop-front in Brewer Street, London, was reproduced from the portfolios of the Society for Photographing Relics of Old London, by the courtesy of Mr. Alfred Marks. Mr. J. C. Traylen, Mr. Ernest Hazell and Mr. Palser considerably assisted the authors by allowing them the use of the drawings bearing their respective names; while to Messrs. Carter and Co. of Poole, Messrs. Singers, and Mr. W. S. Campbell of London, the authors are indebted for the use of the photographs of Plates xxxvii, xlii, and v respectively.

The authors are pleased to have this opportunity of thanking their publisher for valuable help and suggestions throughout the preparation of their book.

HORACE DAN.
E. C. MORGAN WILLMOTT.

CONTENTS.

CHAP.		PAGE.
I	THE OLD SHOP-FRONT (PLATES I-XIII)	1
II	THE ARCHITECTURE OF THE MODERN SHOP-FRONT (PLATES XIV-XXXV)	15
	THE RECESSED SHOP-FRONT	17
	THE TYPE SHOP-FRONT	23
	THE PROJECTING SHOP-FRONT	23
	THE CORNER SHOP	24
	THE DOUBLE-STORIED SHOP-FRONT	25
	THE SHOP-FRONT IN SERIES	28
III	THE PRACTICAL REQUIREMENTS OF THE MODERN SHOP-FRONT (PLATES XXXVI-LII)	30
	MATERIALS	31
	GLAZING	33
	LETTERING	34
	LIGHTING	36
	CONSTRUCTION	38
	STALL-BOARDS AND PAVEMENT LIGHTS	41
	SUN-BLINDS AND ROLLER SHUTTERS	44
	ENTRANCES	46
	CONDENSATION	47

LIST OF PLATES.

CHAPTER I.

PLATE.	
I	Butcher Row, Shrewsbury.
II	No. 34 Haymarket, London.
III	No. 15 Cornhill, London.
IV	Nos. 14A and 14B Brewer Street, London.
V	No. 56 Artillery Row, Aldgate, London.
VI	No. 46 Greek Street, London.
VII	No. 9 Norton Folgate, London.
VIII	No. 181 High Holborn, London.
IX	No. 102 Dean Street, London.
X	No. 4 Market Place, Faversham.
XI	No. 771 High Road, Tottenham.
XII	No. 225 Oxford Street, London.
XIII	No. 102 New Oxford Street, London.

CHAPTER II.

XIV	No. 101 High Holborn, London.
XV	Nos. 108 and 110 High Holborn, London. W. Charles Waymouth, Architect.
XVI	No. 65 St. Paul's Churchyard, London. W. Ernest Hazell, Architect.

PLATE.

XVII No. 25 CHEAPSIDE, LONDON. A. Palser, Architect.

XVIII No. 136 CHEAPSIDE, LONDON.
Read and Macdonald, Architects.

XIX No. 119A PRINCES STREET, EDINBURGH.
Charles E. Dawson, Architect.

XX No. 209 REGENT STREET, LONDON.
T. Kissack, Architect.

XXI No. 212 PICCADILLY, LONDON.
C. R. G. Hall, Architect.

XXII No. 80 GEORGE STREET, EDINBURGH.
John Burnet and Sons, Architects.

XXIII No. 16 BUCHANAN STREET, GLASGOW.
Charles E. Dawson, Architect.

XXIV No. 44 OLD COMPTON STREET, LONDON.

XXV No. 7 PORTUGAL STREET, LONDON.
Horace Field, Architect.

XXVI No. 5 QUEEN VICTORIA STREET, LONDON.
George Walton, Architect.

XXVII No. 83 CHURCH STREET, LIVERPOOL.
T. Myddleton Shallcross, Architect.

XXVIII No. 17 CHARTERHOUSE STREET, LONDON.

XXIX MARKET PLACE, ENFIELD.
Reginald Blomfield, Architect.

XXX No. 10 DOVER STREET, LONDON.
Walter Cave, Architect.

XXXI No. 103 HIGH ROAD, KILBURN, LONDON.

XXXII Nos. 17–37 WIGMORE STREET, LONDON.
Gibson and Wallace, Architects.

XXXIII No. 79 NEW CAVENDISH STREET, MARYLEBONE, LONDON.
George Harvey, Architect.

XXXIV No. 25 HANOVER SQUARE, LONDON.
H. Wackley, Architect.

XXXV Nos. 46–48 LOMBARD STREET, LONDON.

CHAPTER III.

PLATE.

XXXVI Feasegate, York. Penty and Penty, Architects.

XXXVII No. 5 Commercial Street, Bournemouth.

XXXVIII No. 42 Dale Street, Liverpool.
Arnold Ashworth, Architect.

XXXIX Church Street, Liverpool.
Arnold Ashworth, Architect.

XL Nos. 11 and 12, Finsbury Square, London.
C. H. B. Quennell, Architect.

XLI No. 5 Old Bond Street, London.
A. N. Paterson, Architect.

XLII The Singer Manufacturing Co., Paris.

XLIII No. 186 Finchley Road, London.

XLIV No. 225 Finchley Road, London.
Read and Macdonald, Architects.

XLV No. 45 Dover Street.
Blangy and Van Baars, Architects.

XLVI No. 88 Strand, London. W. H. Wuddell, Architect.

XLVII No. 329 Holborn, London.

XLVIII St. Ann's Street, Manchester.
Arnold Ashworth, Architect.

XLIX No. 217 Sauchiehall Street, Glasgow.
Honeyman Keppie and Mackintosh, Architects.

L Argyll Street, Glasgow.

LI Montagne de la Cour, Brussels.
George Walton, Architect.

LII No. 40 West Strand, London.
George Walton, Architect.

LIST OF ILLUSTRATIONS IN THE TEXT.

CHAPTER I.

1. Old Bulk Shop, Clare Market, London . . 2
2. From an old print of Cheapside, London . . 5
3. Old Shop, Abbey Street, Faversham . . face p. 6
4. No. 60 Palace Street, Canterbury . . „ 6
5. No. 137 Long Acre, London . . „ 8
6. Old Shop, Louth, Lincolnshire . . „ 9
7. Saddler's Shop, St. Mary's Street, Stamford . „ 9
8. Jeweller's Shop, High Street, Stamford . . 10
9. Details of Jeweller's Shop, High Street, Stamford . 11
10. Old Shops, Woburn Buildings, London . face p. 12
11. Old Shop, The Butter Market, Canterbury . „ 12
12. Design for a Shop by J. Carter, Architect . . 12
13. Design for a Shop.—Late Eighteenth Century . 14

CHAPTER II.

14. No. 65 St. Paul's Churchyard, London . . 18
15. Section of No. 65 St. Paul's Churchyard, London . 19
16. Section of No. 65 St. Paul's Churchyard, London . 19
17. No. 25 Cheapside, London 21

CHAPTER III.

18. No. 40 West Strand, London . . . 37
19. An Elevation, Plan, etc., of a Typical Shop-Front . 39
20. Section of a Shop-Front 40
21. Section of a Shop-Front 42
22. No. 18 Cockspur Street, London . . . 43
23. Section of Recessed Shop-Front . . . 44
24. Plan of a Shop-Front with Revolving Doors . 47
25. Section of a Shop-Front . . . 48

ENGLISH SHOP-FRONTS
OLD AND NEW

CHAPTER I.

THE OLD SHOP-FRONT.

IT would be hard to state definitely what the first shop-front was like. Historians have been lax in this respect. They have told of sale and of barter, and the historical and geographical causes which made these things possible. Very little information is at hand, however, when enquiry is made as to the character of the buildings or shops, from which the early merchants sold or exchanged their commodities.

The first and primitive shop was probably a simple movable trading booth, capable of being easily taken down, and carried from this place to that, and structurally only just strong enough for such buffetings of weather as it might be expected to withstand in the open places of the markets. For in early times the fair and the open market were the chief means of effective retail trading. Even in this, the twentieth century, the lack of progressiveness upon the part of the authorities concerned is responsible for the continuance of many street markets in London ; markets which are as primitive in their form and appurtenances as the booths of the early merchants. That many of the most cultured and civilized of the early nations exhibited the same indifference to their shopping places must be admitted, for the stories of their times as deduced by antiquarians and archæologians seem to indicate that the Venetians, the Egyptians, the Assyrians, and even such a nation of traders as the Carthagenians, all had nothing more substantial to trade from than the most primitive wooden booths. At Pompeii, however, there are sufficient remains to indicate that a large number of shops in this ancient and populous city were built of brick and stone. In the house of Pansa it is possible there were three shops, with the remains of counters and dwarf walls, evidently for the storage of goods. Besides this, staircase remains suggest that the shops had apartments over. There were two other shops, one evidently a baker's, as a bakehouse is attached, and the other a corner shop with splayed corner entrance, large windows and attached stores.

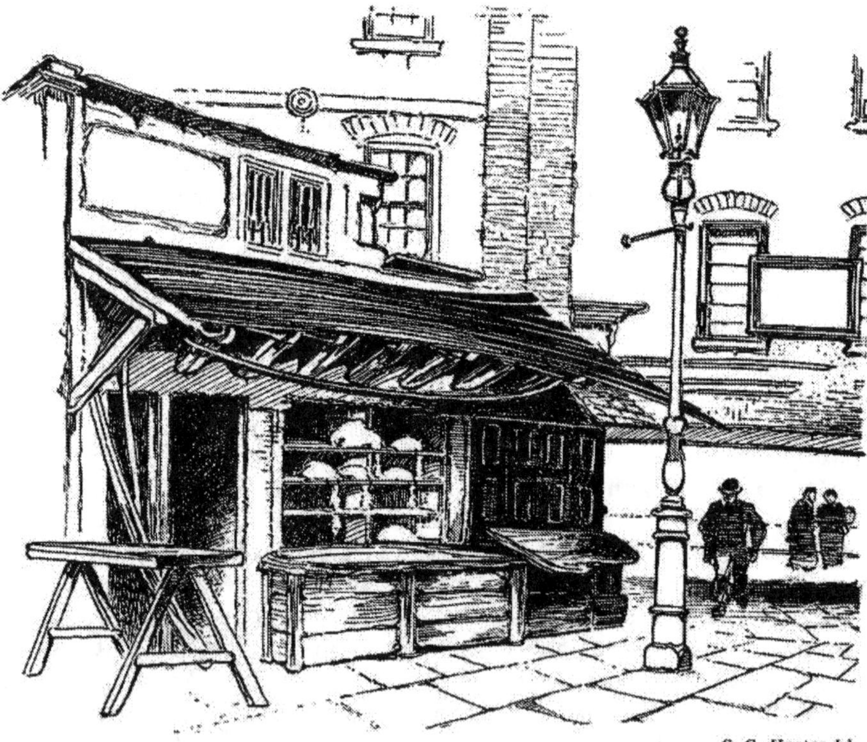

C. G. Harper del.

Fig. 1. OLD BULK SHOP, CLARE MARKET, LONDON.

The trading booth of the old world must have remained unchanged and unimproved until the middle ages, when a certain progression is noticeable, insomuch as the shop, instead of being a temporary structure, became a permanent part of the building. It was, however, still unpretentious and relatively unimportant. At first it was merely an opening and simple framework filled at night with shutters. It may or may not have been glazed, as, although glass according to Bede was introduced into England as early as 674

A.D., it was not generally known of until about 1180. Even then it was but sparingly used, being expensive to procure and fix. The shop opening was sometimes closed at night with a wooden shutter hinged to the frame of the window. In the daytime this shutter was let down and rested upon a wooden leg or bracket, the flat table thus formed being used for the display of the goods.

From the first mediæval shop was developed other types which appropriately enough were termed Bulk Shops, and which were more prominently noticeable in London. The inset sketch (Fig. 1), is a reproduction of one of these early fronts. This was a poulterer's shop in Gilbert's Passage, Clare Market, W.C. It was destroyed in 1878, and was the last existing shop of its type. An old act of 1666 (believed to have been drawn up by Wren) has some curious enactments with relation to shop-fronts which doubtless prompted the development and largely affected the construction of these ancient Bulk Shops. "For conveniency of shops . . . no bricks, jetties, windows, posts, or anything of the like sort, shall be made or erected in any streets, lanes, or by-lanes, to extend beyond the ancient foundations, nor that any house be set further into the street than the ancient foundations, *saving only* that in the high and principal streets it shall be lawful for the inhabitants to suffer their stall-boards (when their shop windows are set open) to turn over and extend 11in. and no more from the foundations of their houses into the street for the better conveniency of their shop windows."

It will be seen on reference to the illustration that the hinged shutter has become the top of a fixed and permanent base, while an overhanging pent roof (the result of a further enactment of the 1666 act which required the erection of such a roof over the footpath) projected over the bulk upon which the shutter rested when down. These bulks at night became the hard and uncomfortable, though at least weather protected couches of the homeless and bedless of London in the early days of the seventeenth century.

Plate i is an illustration of a fifteenth century shop-front from Shrewsbury, and it is very fortunate that such an example still remains to show the class of shop erected during the Tudor period. It will be noticed that this front is entirely in wood, but it is known that there were also carried out during the fifteenth century a considerable number of shop-fronts in stone. In the example illustrated the entire building is in half-timber work, the upper portions of the building projecting out one above the other. In the stone fronts a wide arch usually spanned the main opening, which had a side entrance. From this a staircase led to the "solar" over. Seldom, though, were such stern materials as stone or brick employed for shop-fronts, and with the accession of Elizabeth the adaptation of wood and half-timber for both shop-front and building became generally prevalent.

At Chester certain local conditions were responsible for a type of double storied shops, which were known and famed as the "Chester Rows." Amongst modern writers there exists considerable difference of opinion as to their origin. In certain portions of Chester, notably Foregate Street and Watergate Street (South), the upper storey of the building projected out so considerably over the lower storey that props or columns were required to be placed upon the pavement edge in order to support the projecting superstructure. This created a collonade, artistic and useful, and these shops became the prototype of the modern idea, carried out in stone at the Rue de Rivoli and certain other streets in Paris; also at the Ritz Hotel, London. Of the advantages of the Rows the writer in "Vale Royal" notices the most obvious, for he says, describing them, "that a man may go dry from one place of the city to another, and never come into the street, but go as it were into galleries, which they call the Roes; which have shops on both sides, and underneath, with divers fair stairs to go up or down the street." Another writer, Dr. Brushfield, notices only their defects, for he says "that the Shops are all so dark and close that a Stranger riding thro' can see none; and 'tis otherwise very incommodious."

It is a matter for regret that it is not possible to include an illustration of a Jacobean shop-front. The last of these, and an excellent example from Exeter, was destroyed some two years ago. Generally speaking, however, they possessed no distinguishing characteristics of form or plan, though decoratively they may possibly have been interesting. Indeed it is easy to believe that the designers of those times thought enough of the shop-front to give it that elaborate richness of effect which made the adjuncts of their buildings so architecturally abnormal. In the smaller towns and villages during the seventeenth century, the marked tendency in domestic work to overhang the several upper stories of the buildings was directly responsible for small projecting oriel shops supported on brackets. Sometimes these small bays were roofed with a simple little pent roof, but more often they modestly

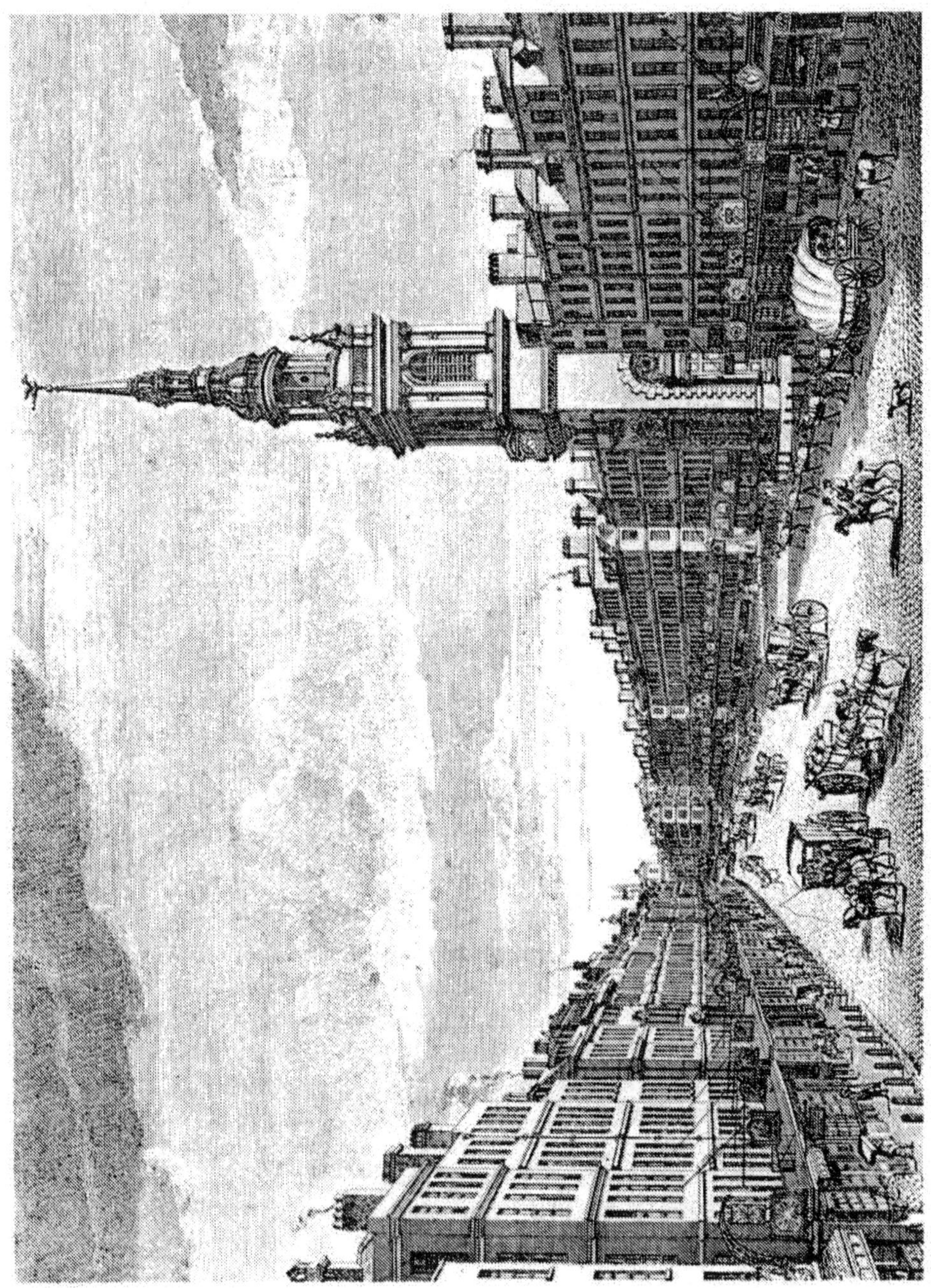

Fig. 2. FROM AN OLD PRINT OF CHEAPSIDE, LONDON.

hid themselves under the concealing soffit of an upper projecting storey.

Many such projecting oriel shop-fronts are shown in the old print of Cheapside, or West Cheap as it was originally called (Figure 2), the date of which is about 1700.

These oriel bays gradually became more important and more obtrusive. They were given a good projection into the street, a permanent base instead of the simple wooden bracket of their earlier support, and on occasions, a large covering lean-to roof. Indeed they finally projected them so far on to the paths and pavements as to constitute a nuisance to traffic and an inconvenience to pedestrians. It may possibly be because of this that a bye-law made at the end of the seventeenth century limited the projection of bow or bay windows to 10in. in a public place and 5in. in a byepath or lane. A natural result of the passing of this bye-law was the creation of the delicately flat projecting bow windows which were such a marked feature of the Queen Anne and succeeding periods. Figure 3 is an illustration of an old shop-front at Faversham. Its simplicity of form and detail are excellent, and it is a fair illustration of the type of shop-front which evolved itself from the projecting oriel shops mentioned above.

The eighteenth century was a remarkable time in so far as the development of shop-fronts was concerned. With the accession of George I the distributive industries of the country seemed to become suddenly imbued with a revolutionary progressiveness, which, until the time of William IV, was responsible for the erection of an extraordinary number of shop-fronts of good architectural character. Indeed, in a consideration of the work of this period, a permanent feeling of regret is felt that the conditions of business life have so changed, as to render commercially ineffective the need of the further creation of such excellent old shop-fronts as the famous tobacconists in the Haymarket, London (Plate ii). Surely amongst many old fronts that are interesting, many that are quaint, none are more suggestive of refinement, and of that excellent proportion of form and detail, which are all the essentials of a precise architectural effectiveness. Note the charming fanlight to the doors with their radiating glazing bars, the excellent detail of the frieze and cornice and even the successful architectural modesty of the doors. This front is especially interesting insomuch as it seems fairly certain that it was originally designed for the set purposes of the

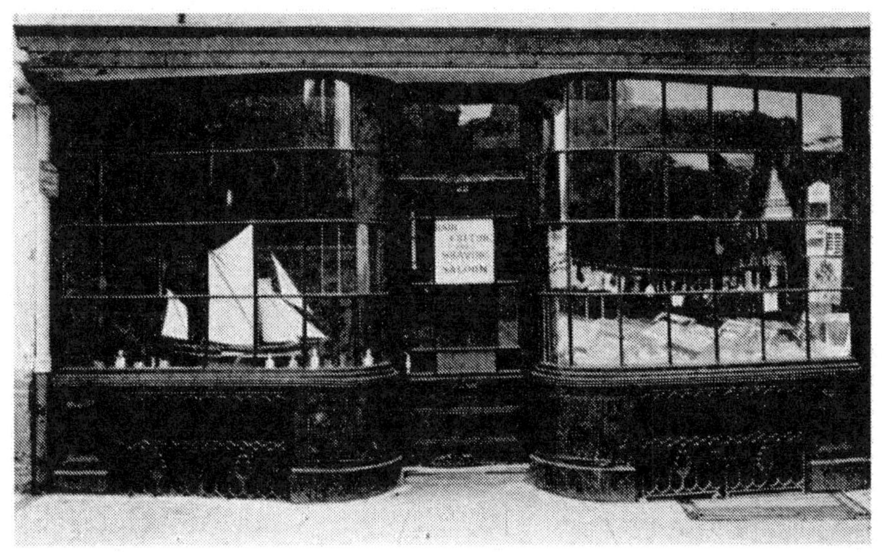

Fig. 3. OLD SHOP, ABBEY STREET, FAVERSHAM.

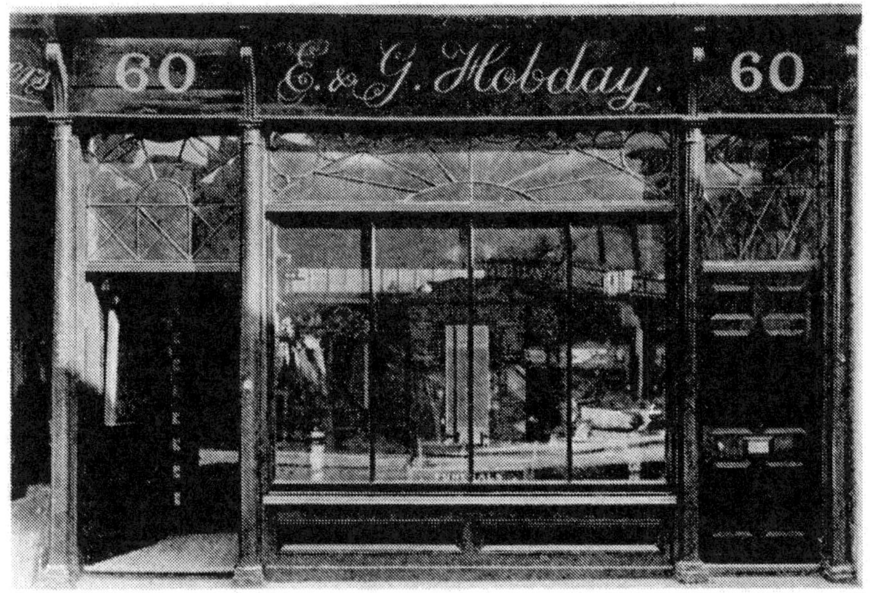

Fig. 4. NO. 60 PALACE STREET, CANTERBURY.

business of a tobacco and snuff merchant. The date is about 1770.

Plate iii is an illustration of the oldest shop-front still existing in the city of London. It is often referred to as "The Little Green Shop in Cornhill," but is still better known as "Birch's." For a good many years the interesting and delicate carving gracing the spandrels and mullions of the simple three-light window was hidden by the paint which many generations had applied year by year. Recently, however, all these coats of paint—it is estimated there were about two hundred—were burnt and scraped off. The carving thus revealed is of considerable merit and suggests that the shop might possibly have been erected during the Adams period. It is asserted, however, that this little front was built quite a hundred years before this time; probably during the reign of George I. The original proprietor was one Samuel Horton who was afterwards joined by a Samuel Birch. The latter was Lord Mayor of London, 1815, and had some reputation as a dramatist and verse writer. He was nicknamed "Mr. Pattyman" because of his connection with the pastry-cook business. About 1830 this business became and still continues the property of Messrs. Ring and Brymer, the well-known caterers.

In the example from Brewer Street, London (Plate iv), probably an early eighteenth century design, the treatment is somewhat exceptional. At the same time it marks a step in the development of shop-front designing. Here the architect has cast aside the shackles of an already born and already fettering commercial predication and boldly adopted for the decoration of a shop premises, an imperfectly understood, but in this case perfectly adapted Renaissance inspiration.

Plate v is probably contemporary with the Brewer Street example, the heavy character of the detail in each being very similar. In the example from Artillery Row the general effect is, however, much richer. The good architectural treatment of the two doorways is distinctive of a design for a shop-front, which, while owing much to its classic form and details, owes more to the clever and original manner of their adaptation. Such a front as this is worthy of the highest praise.

The example from Greek Street, Soho (Plate vi), while not laying claim to any great distinction is still of more than average interest. There is something potently effective in the charming, though somewhat rustic bareness of the simple Ionic columns.

Although the fronts of the eighteenth century are considerably varied, yet there are certain marked characteristics common to them all. The windows, for instance, are almost invariably divided up into squares by means of moulded glazing bars, these bars becoming lighter in form as time advanced. Indeed, in shop-fronts, their most reliable guide in regard to date is the heaviness or lightness of the woodwork details. Thus the shop-fronts of the nineteenth century are more refined and delicate than the sturdy and perhaps more architectural fronts of the seventeenth or eighteenth centuries. Semi-circular fanlights decorated with radiating and curved glazing bars are very common. Cornices and pilasters are very much alike in the manner of their use, the enrichments however being plentifully varied. Most of the fronts are refined and well proportioned, due recognition having been given to the limited uses of the material, the latter being invariably wood. A classic influence upon the nature of the mouldings and details is quite pronounced. Thin pilasters are used a great deal. These are usually without caps of any kind. Often they are recessed or fluted or simply panelled.

In form or plan absence of any limitation in regard to straightness of frontage, is always sure to produce the effective and characteristic bowing of the main window. The stall-boards are usually pretty high. Sometimes they are panelled in wood and very often additionally protected by some excellent wrought ironwork of good character and design. Bead-butt and bead-flush doors are greatly in favour, while sliding shutters are sometimes used in preference to the clumsy hinged boards of the previous century.

The chemist's shop from Norton Folgate, London (Plate vii), is an excellent example of these distinctions of form and detail, which were the guiding characteristics of the shop-fronts of the eighteenth century. Besides this, however, the design has a charm and grace of its own, a charm no doubt extracted from the individuality of its clever designer. What a centralizing and enriching effect too, the capitally modelled eagle has upon the effectiveness of the composition.

Plate viii has many of the merits attached to the Haymarket front, viz: directness, suitability, and restraint. The curved centre portion is a pleasing variation, and at the same time a typical variation of plan. The carved brackets each side of the doors are simple and honest.

Plate ix is a remarkably clever and interesting design. Artis-

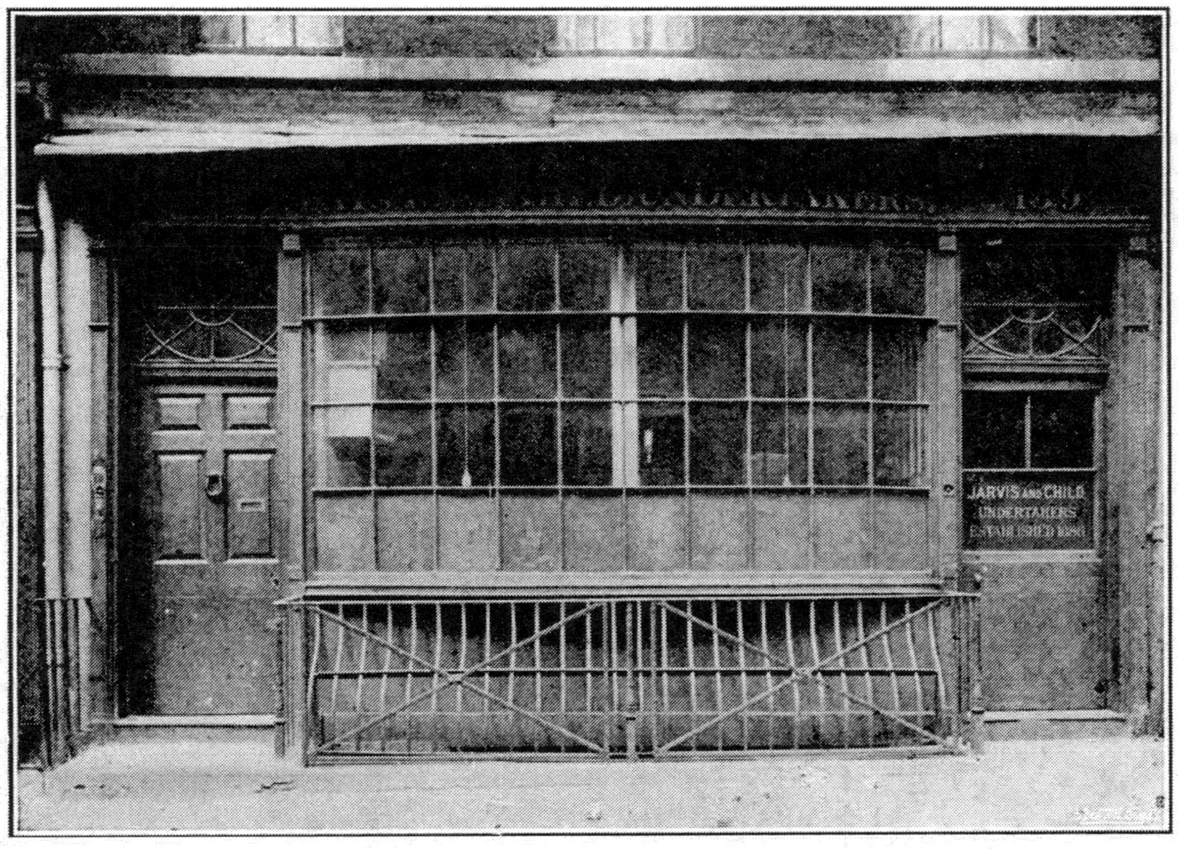

Fig. 5. NO. 137 LONG ACRE, LONDON.

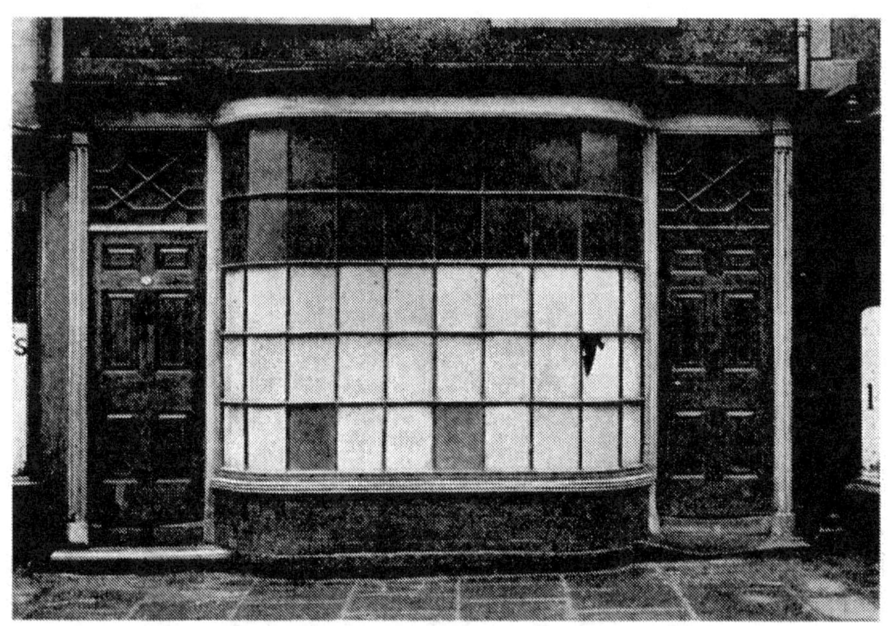

Fig. 6. OLD SHOP, LOUTH, LINCOLNSHIRE.

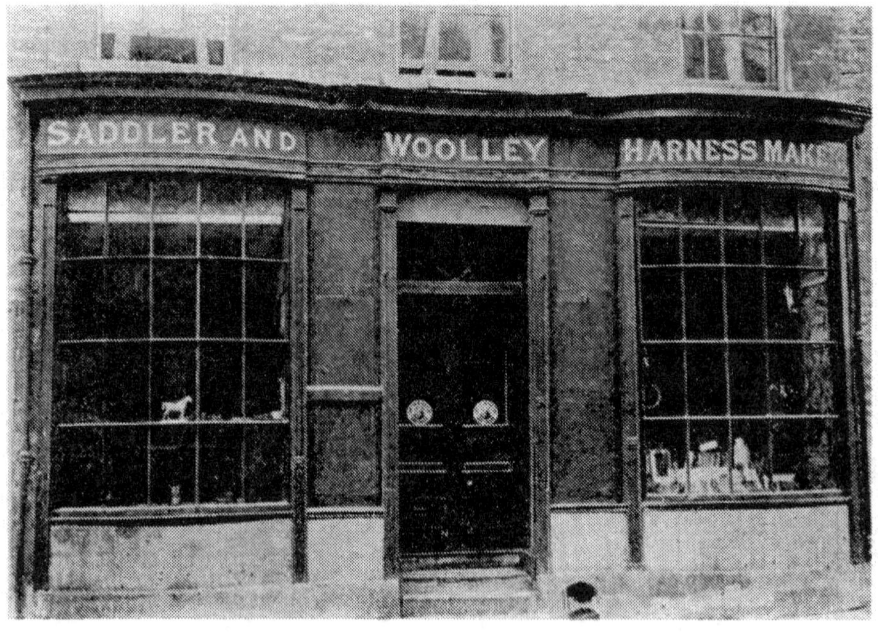

Fig. 7. SADDLER'S SHOP, ST. MARY'S STREET, STAMFORD.

tically its merits are too obvious to need any encouraging commentary from the writer. Surely, though, too much praise cannot be given to the excellent proportioning and balancing of all the parts, the careful distribution of voids and solids, and the pleasing and logical recognition of the trite value of a curve properly transposed against the necessary straight.

The Canterbury example (Figure 4) is in some respects not unlike Plate ix. In both the architect has cultivated that originality which can find easy expression in quaintly curved and varied glazing bars. Figure 5, although not especially distinctive, calls for illustration if only by reason of the careful refinement of its very characteristic detail.

It will be opportune, perhaps, to here note the good character of the lettering in most of these fronts, and it is a natural reversion of thought from this to a characteristic of the mediæval shop-front. In the latter the shopkeeper sought for some quiet, often artistic, always quaint, and never vulgar advertisement in curiously devised signs which proclaimed his calling and the goods he sold. Lombard Street, London, is very famous in this connection, and it is easy to picture this street as it appeared with its hundreds of hanging signs. Besant describes the signs of old London as a nuisance. He tells us that the many pranks of wind and rain so rusted the bearings of their hinges, that the musical symphonies they rendered at nights, were an intolerable nuisance to the peaceful citizen. That most of these signs have disappeared, and that none of the early Victorian fronts possessed them is easily explained by the fact that an act passed about 1667 prohibited the projection of them into the streets. The old print of Cheapside (Figure 2) shows many old and interesting signs.

Figure 6 is a front from Louth in Lincolnshire. Many such are still existing in the country, and although neither elaborated by detail or made architecturally obtrusive by form, they have a quiet and pleasing dignity of their own which exemplifies the need of their modest good qualities being properly appreciated.

The saddler's shop from Stamford (Figure 7) is one of the many fronts in this town, which has helped to contribute largely to a correct historical knowledge of the work of the later Renaissance. It is probably earlier in date than the two fronts last described. Especially pleasing in this design is the satisfactory spacing of the three windows of the superstructure over the shop openings and

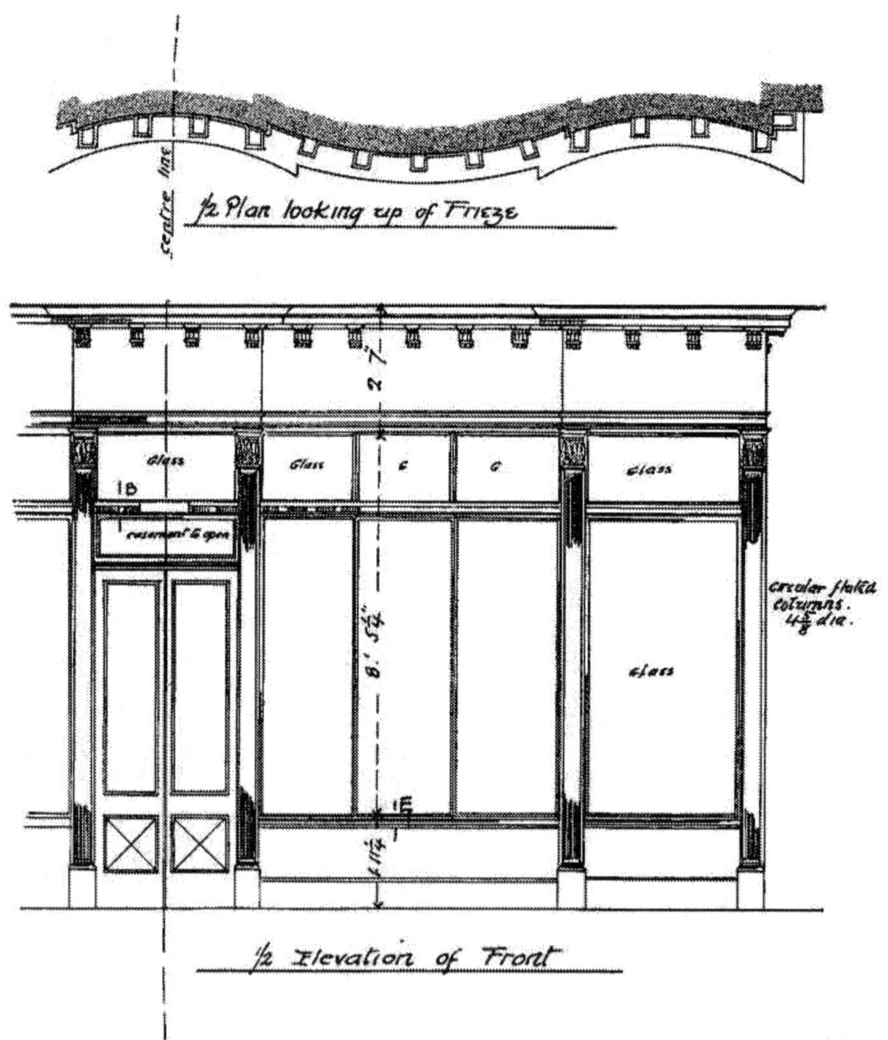

Fig. 8. JEWELLER'S SHOP, HIGH ST., STAMFORD.

J. C. Traylen del.

door. Evidently the designer appreciated to the full the need of the two solid piers either side of the entrance; these giving much strength and excellent balance to the composition.

The confectioner's shop from Faversham (Plate x) is quite a typical design, but the general character of the detail is scarcely so refined as other fronts of a like character which have been illustrated. Originally the bowed window was glazed in small panes of glass.

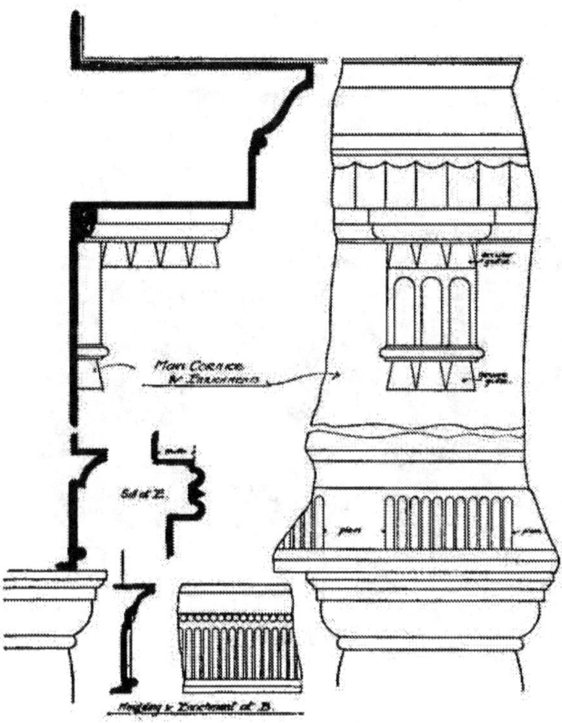

Fig. 9. DETAILS OF JEWELLER'S SHOP, HIGH STREET, STAMFORD.

J. C. Traylen del.

The measured drawing of Sims, Jeweller (Figure 8) is another Stamford shop, very similar to that already described. The details (Figure 9), however, are somewhat different, and the general effect is not so vigorous by reason of the larger amount of glass area.

Plate xi, a projecting front, though largely spoilt by the modern lead glazing of the front door, is still interesting by reason of the necessities which produce its form. One of the many brooks in the neighbourhood of London known as the Moselle often overflowed and flooded the adjacent houses. The floors of the latter were accordingly kept high, and many steps leading to the front door had to be provided for. The brook was afterwards culverted, and here shops are now built over it.

The series of old fronts shown in Figure 10 all project upon small wooden corbel brackets. They were probable erected towards the end of the eighteenth or the beginning of the nineteenth century. The illustration demonstrates the value of the picturesque even in shop-front designing. For here, how charming is the pleasing break in the planes of surface occasioned by the curved projecting windows. The wrought-iron balconies are also not without their value in the artistic interest of the whole.

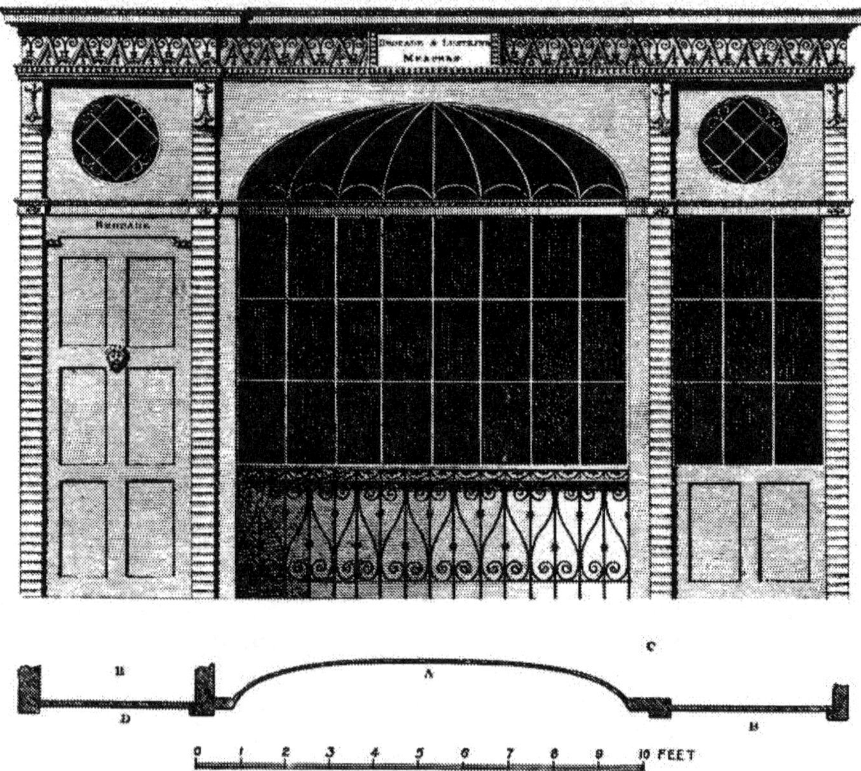

Figure 12. DESIGN FOR A SHOP BY J. CARTER, ARCHITECT.

Plate xii is another shop-front which aptly indicates the value of the glazing bar as a decorative accessory to the front, and a pretty emphasis of the goods of certain trades. Apart from the simple refinement of the woodwork details, it is hard to miss noticing how successfully the glazing bars frame the goods contained in the window. We must not miss, either, the excellent shuttered and bead-flush door and the iron stall-board balusters.

Figure 11 differs only from the typical fronts of the latter part

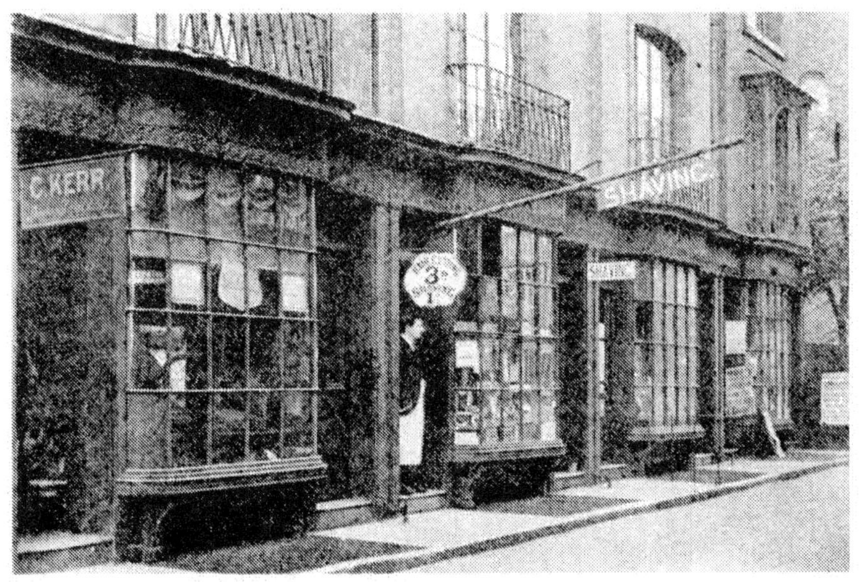

Fig. 10. OLD SHOPS, WOBURN BUILDINGS, LONDON.

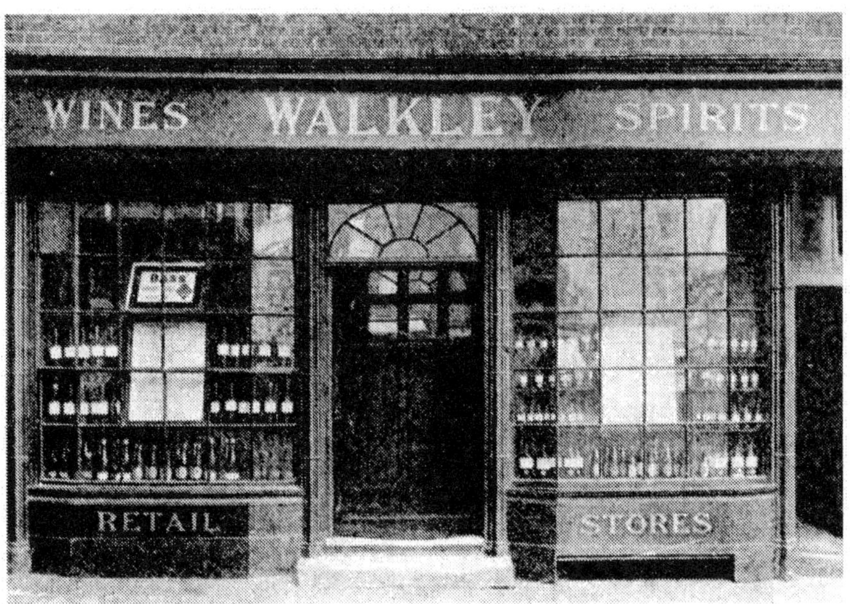

Fig. 11. OLD SHOP, THE BUTTER MARKET, CANTERBURY.

of the eighteenth century insomuch as the architect, in preference to the more common bowed form, has reverted to the alignment of an ordinary bay window.

We have pleasure in including a reproduction of a shop-front by J. Carter, the probable date of which is about 1774 (Figure 12). Here the architect, with a pleasing desire for originality, has reversed the usual procedure and bowed his shop-window inwards instead of outwards. Obviously, however, this could have been only done for some little æsthetic effect, for the small recessed space thus obtained is not used for standing in, but is shut off by means of iron railings.

Figure 13 is a reproduction of a design for a shop-front taken from a series of designs of shop-fronts and door-cases published by J. Taylor at the Architectural Library, No. 56, Holborn, London, probably about the end of the eighteenth century. The design is an admirable example of the more orthodox adoption of classic forms in relation to the designing of shop-fronts. The surface planes of the front are pleasingly broken, while the detail, if conventional, is generally of a good character.

With the accession to the throne of Queen Victoria, the thoughtful and excellent work of Nash and the other architects of the Stucco period was responsible for some good shop-front designs, a typical example being illustrated by Plate xiii. It is very noticeable how much they differ from the eighteenth century work; more especially in regard to the adoption of a certain orthodoxy in the use of Classic Orders and their accompanying details. This example known as "Laws," Oxford Street, was especially designed for that firm in 1849, and it is interesting to note that the architect was not confined by the client to the "all glass" treatment, which even at this time was becoming the recognized treatment for a shop-front. Because of this, and because of the fact that the building was designed as one complete whole, there is a considerable success in the heavy Classic columns with the simple bowed windows in between.

The Great Exhibition of 1851 must, for purposes of this book, be the dividing line between the old shop-front and the new. For this great gathering was revolutionary in its effect upon social, political, and industrial life. A useful prominence was given to the encouragement of the minor arts and crafts; those arts and crafts such as glass-making, which were largely responsible for the great change which afterwards became noticeable in shop-front designing.

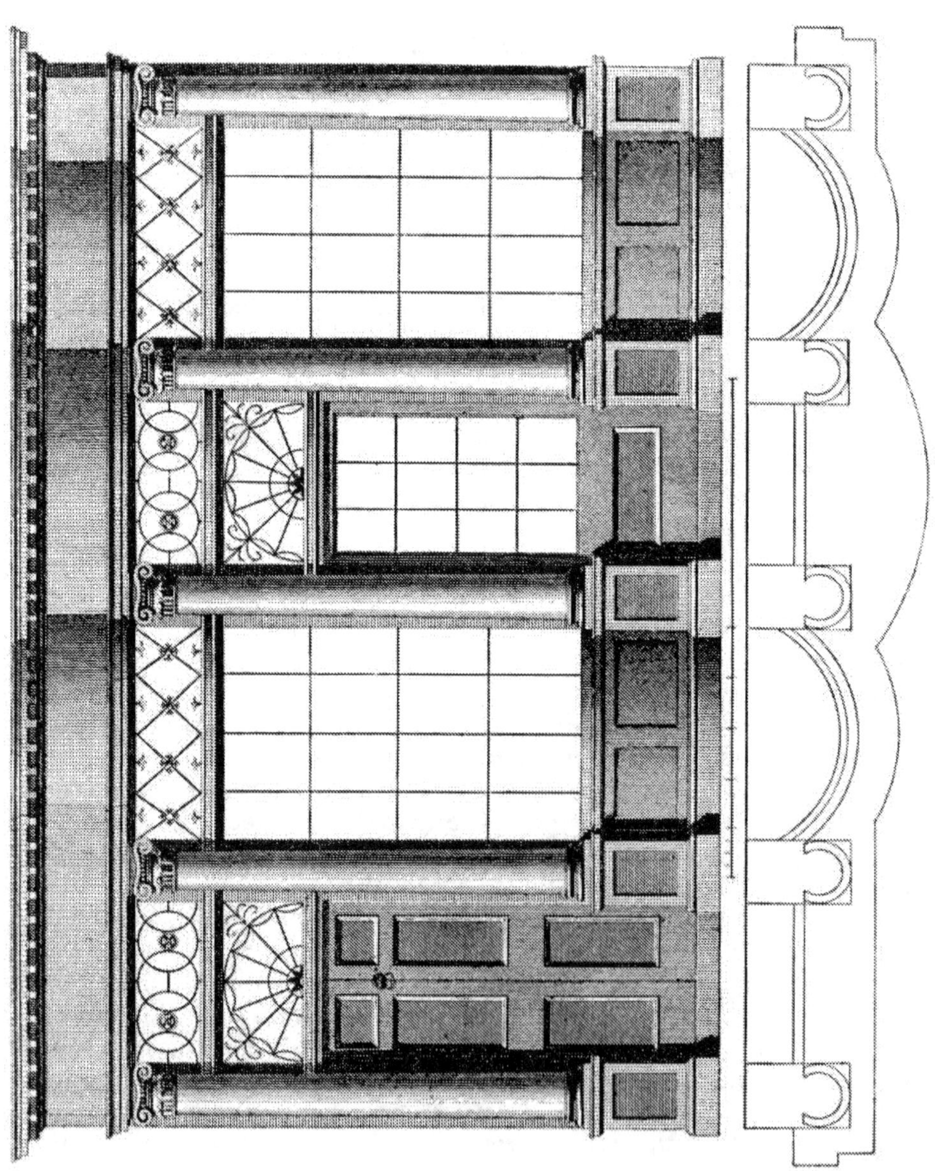

Figure 13. DESIGN FOR A SHOP.—LATE EIGHTEENTH CENTURY.

Plate 1.

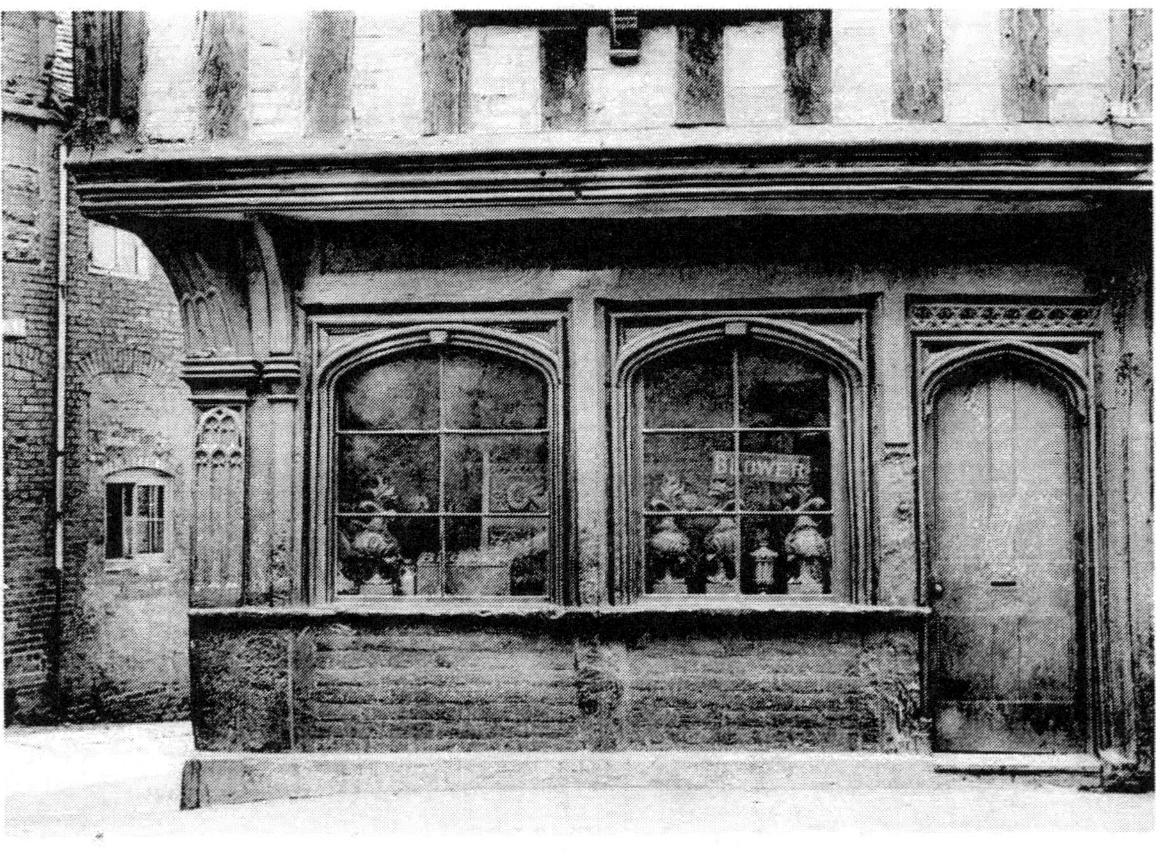

BUTCHER ROW, SHREWSBURY.

Plate 2.

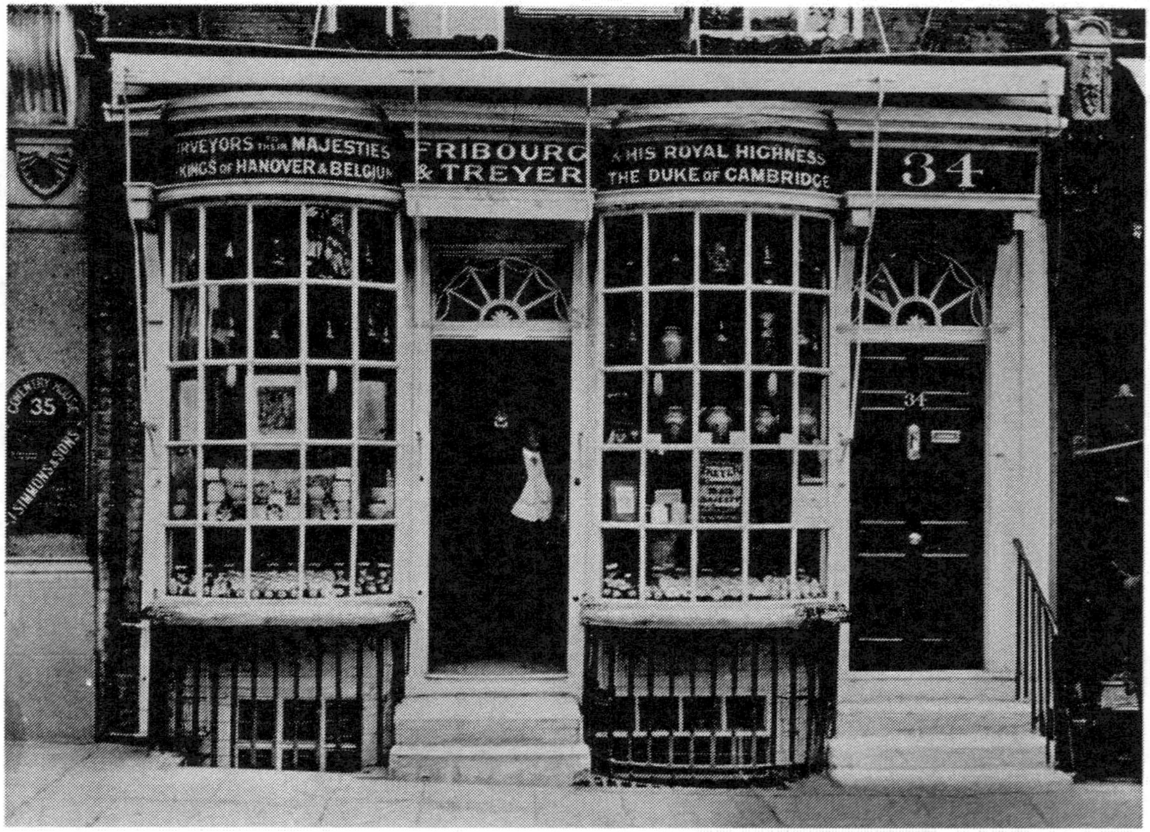

NO. 34, HAYMARKET, LONDON.

Plate 3.

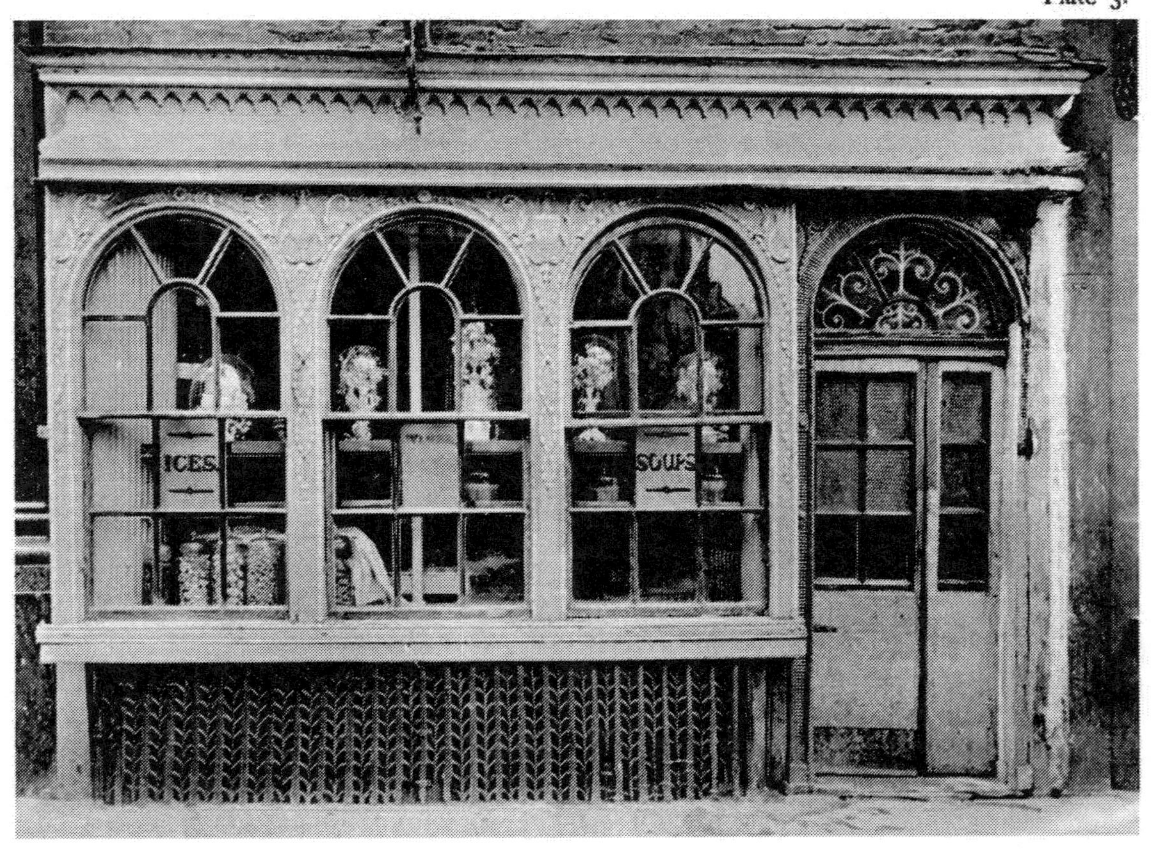

NO. 15, CORNHILL, LONDON.

Plate 4.

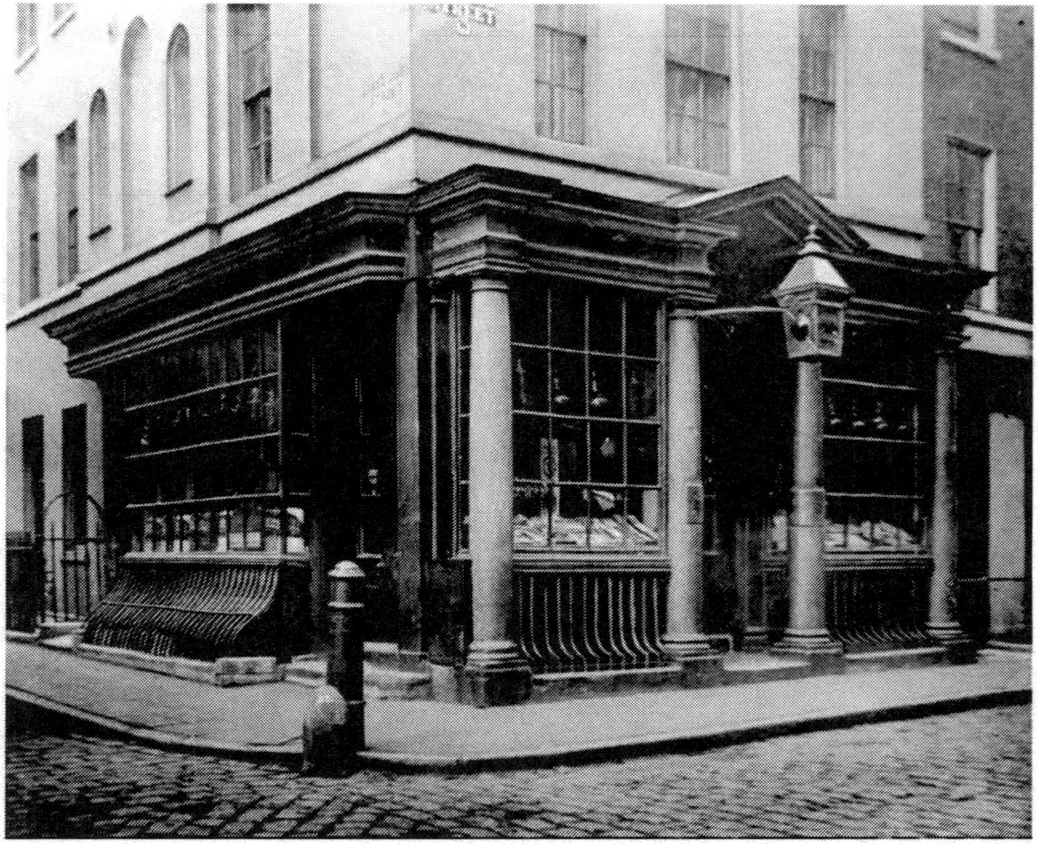

NOS. 14A & 14B, BREWER STREET, LONDON.

Plate 5.

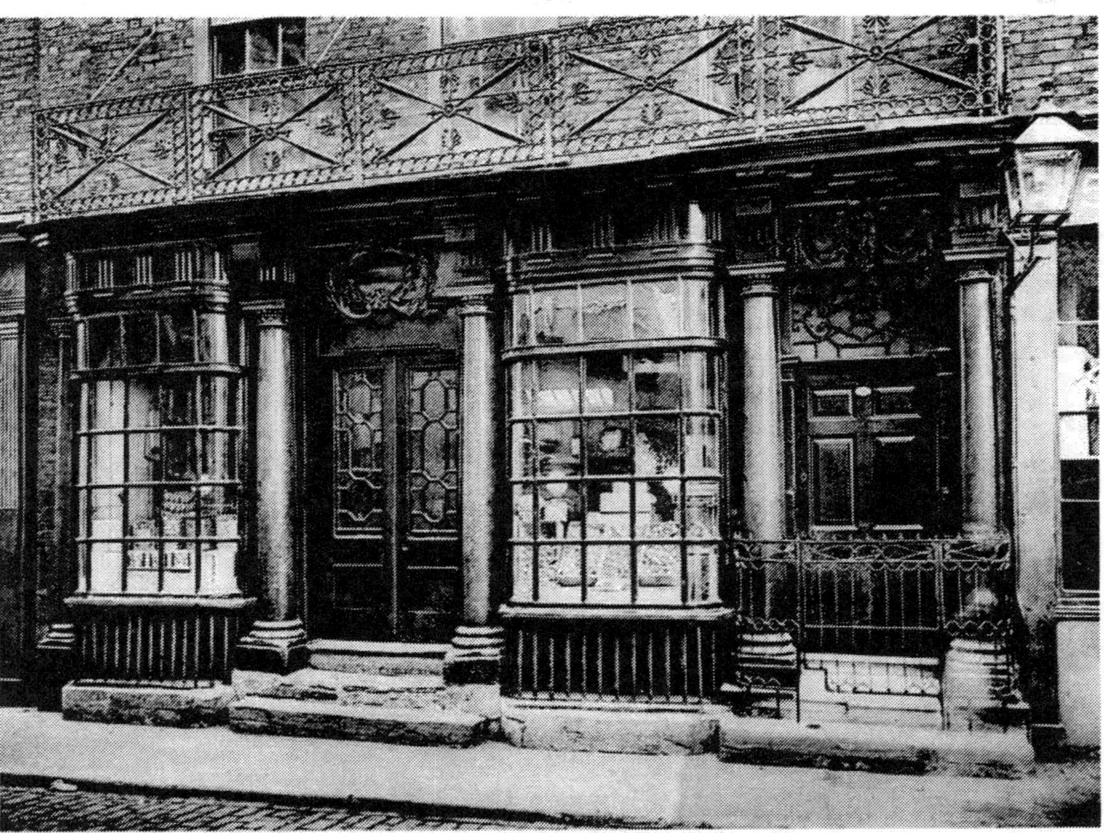

NO. 56, ARTILLERY LANE, ALDGATE, LONDON.

Plate 6.

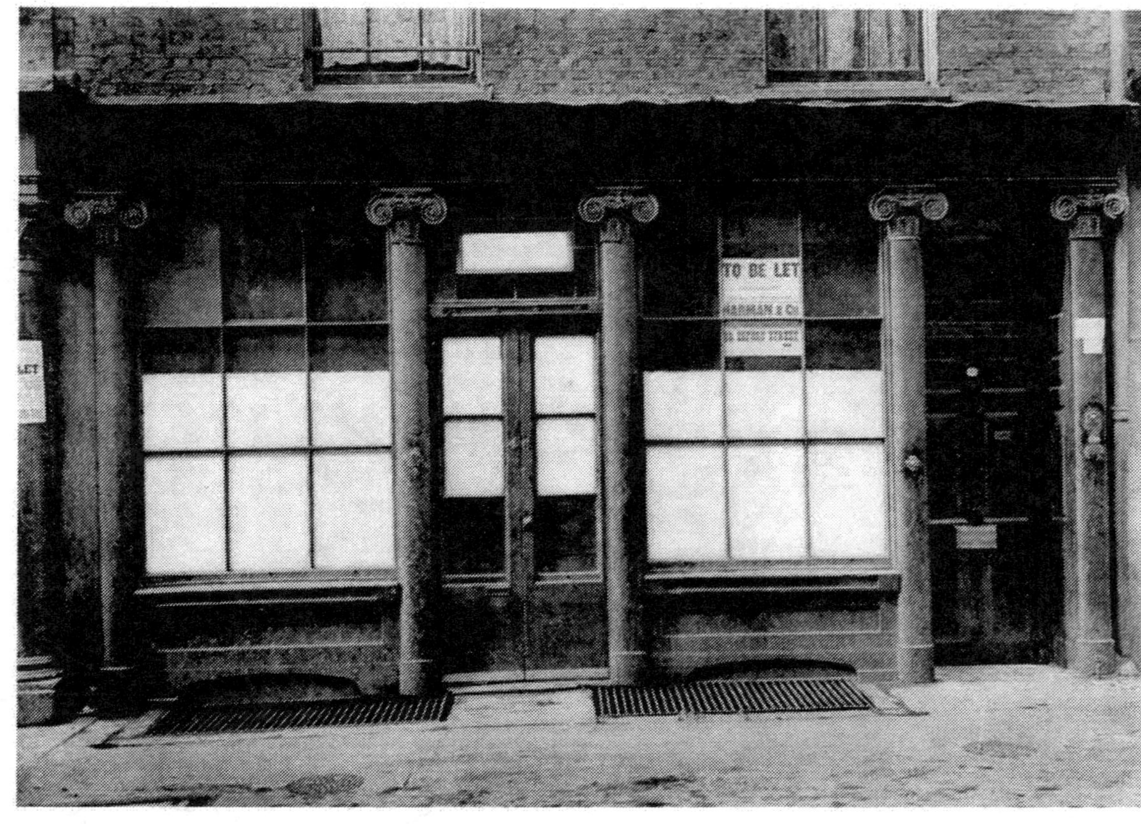

No. 46, GREEK STREET, LONDON.

Plate 7.

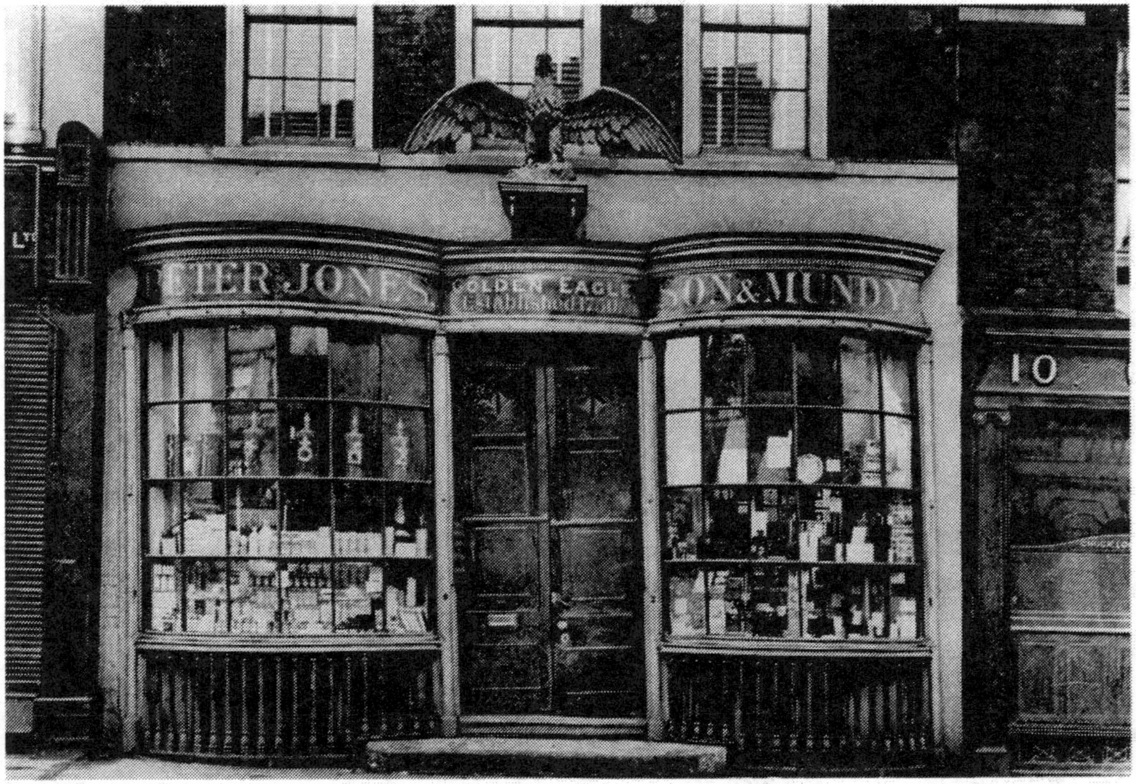

NO. 9, NORTON FOLGATE, ALDGATE, LONDON.

Plate 8.

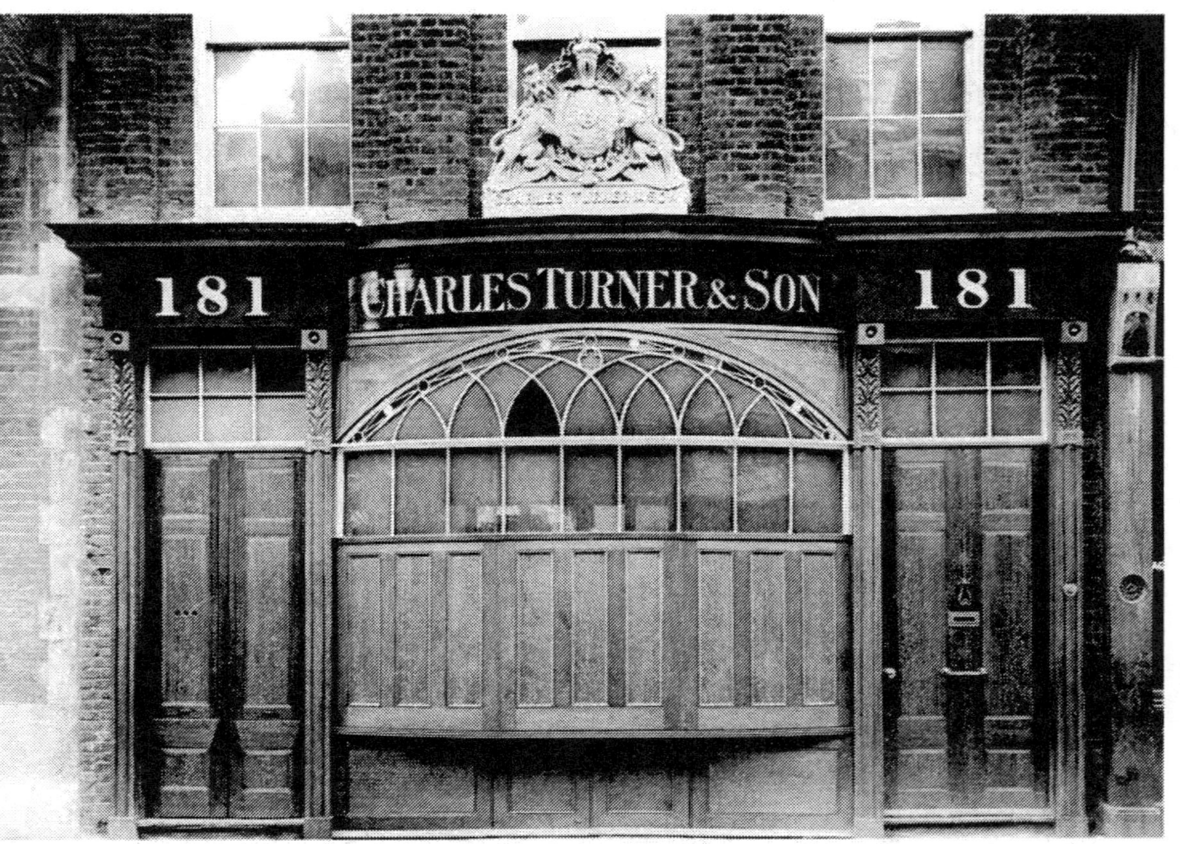

NO. 181, HIGH HOLBORN, LONDON.

Plate 9.

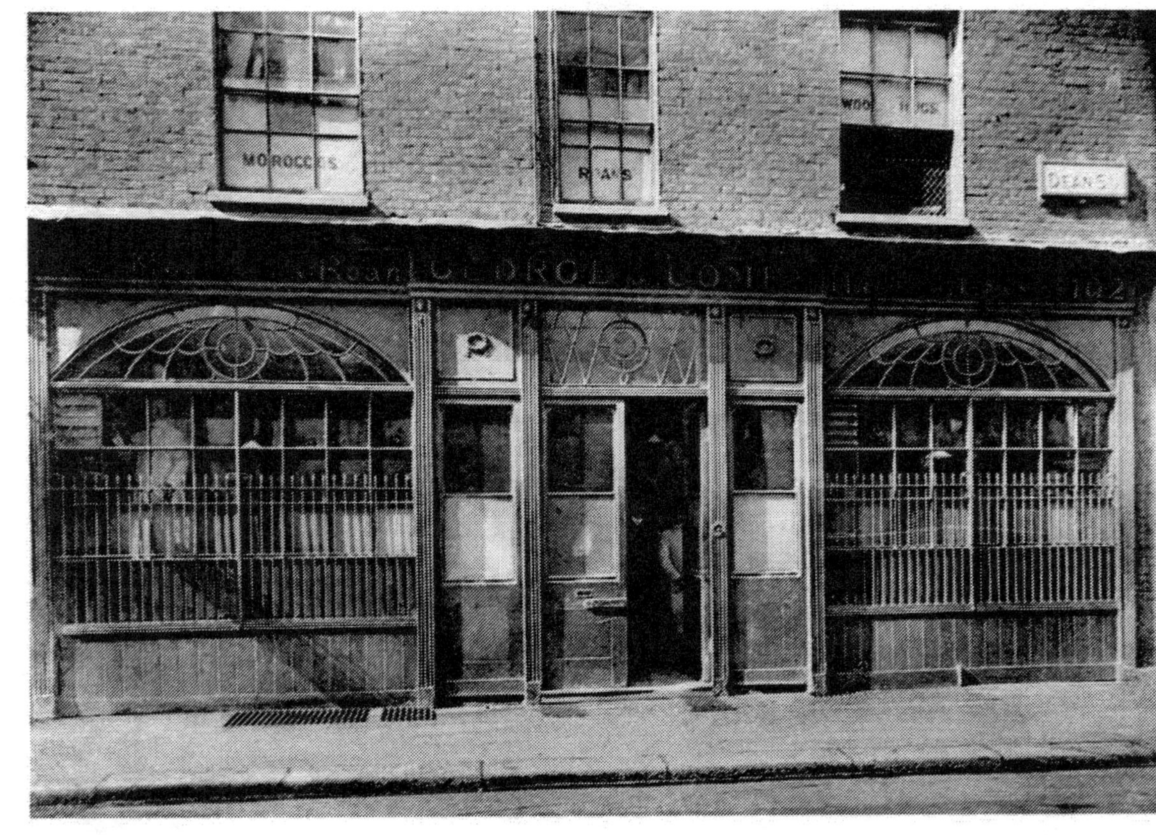

NO. 102, DEAN STREET, SOHO, LONDON.

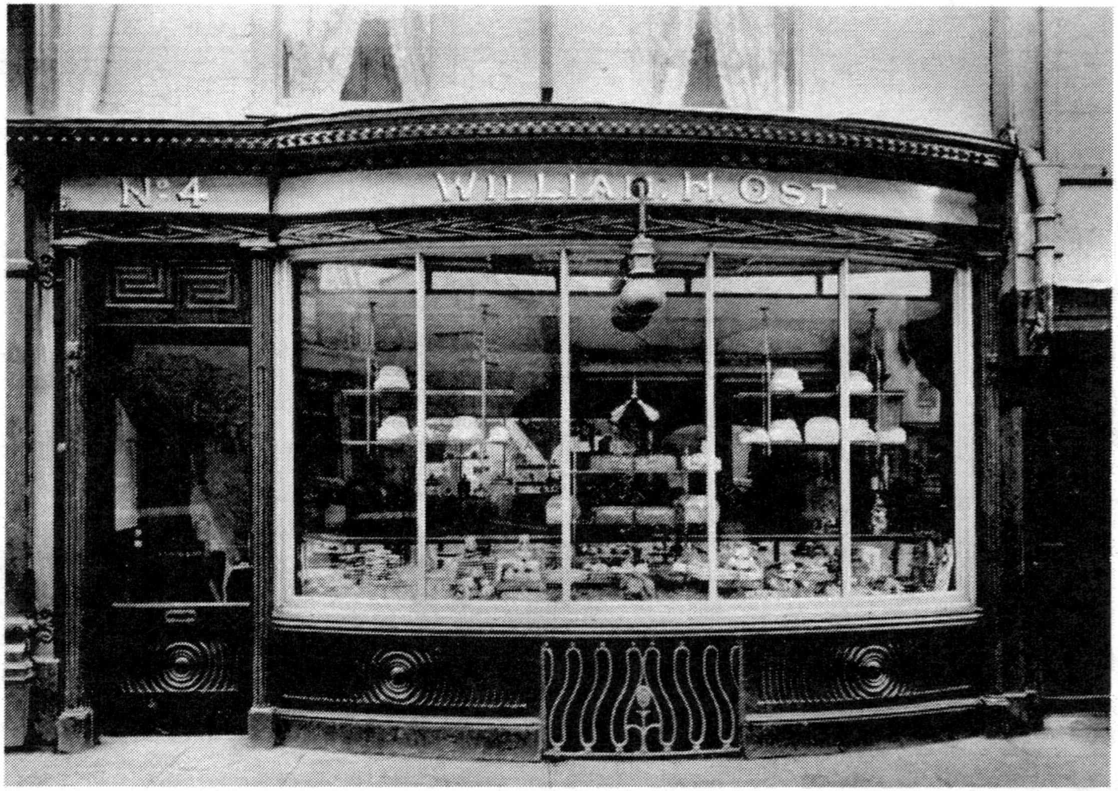

Plate 10.

NO. 4, MARKET PLACE, FAVERSHAM.

Plate 11.

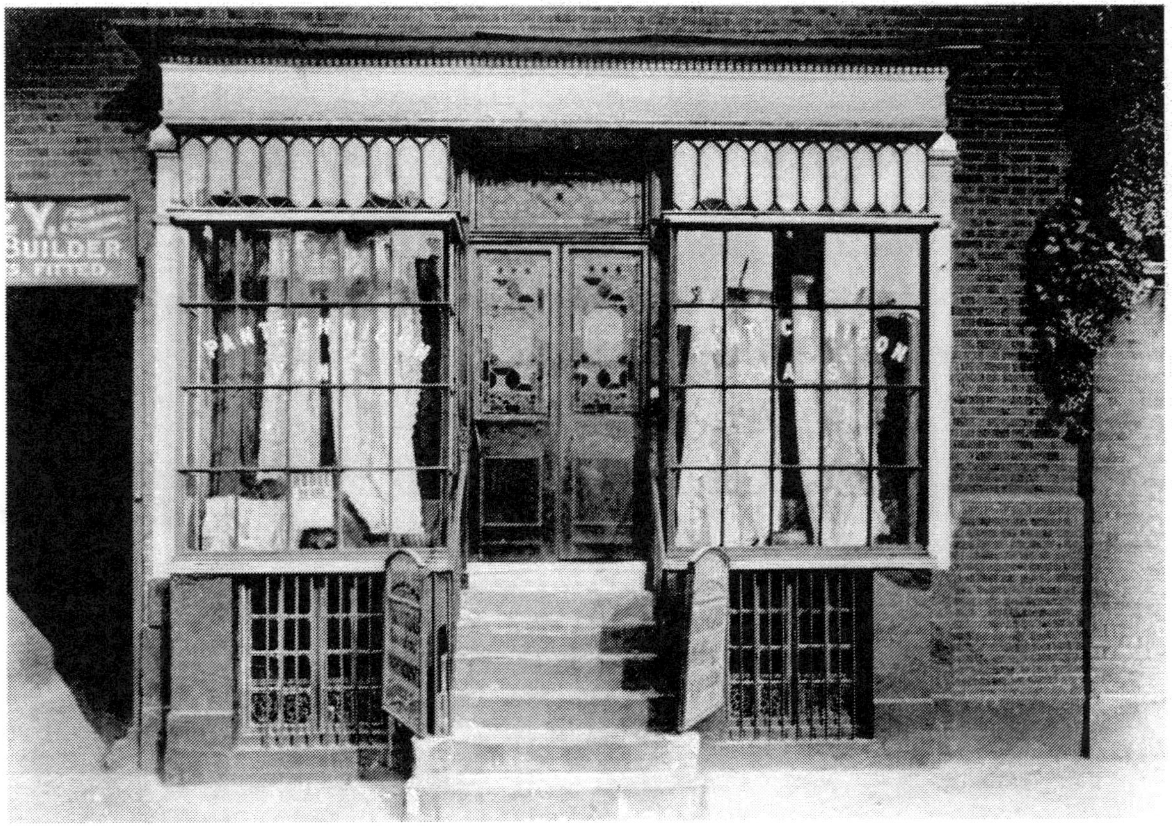

NO. 771, HIGH ROAD, TOTTENHAM.

Plate 12.

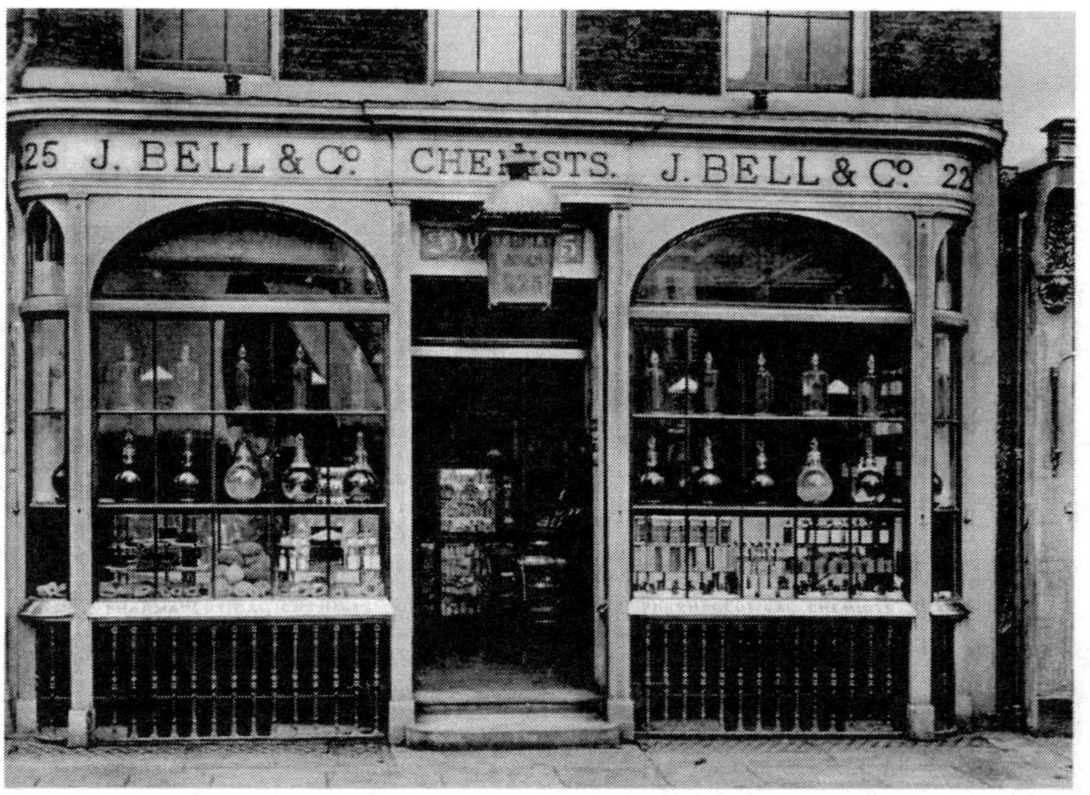

NO. 225, OXFORD STREET, LONDON.

Plate 13.

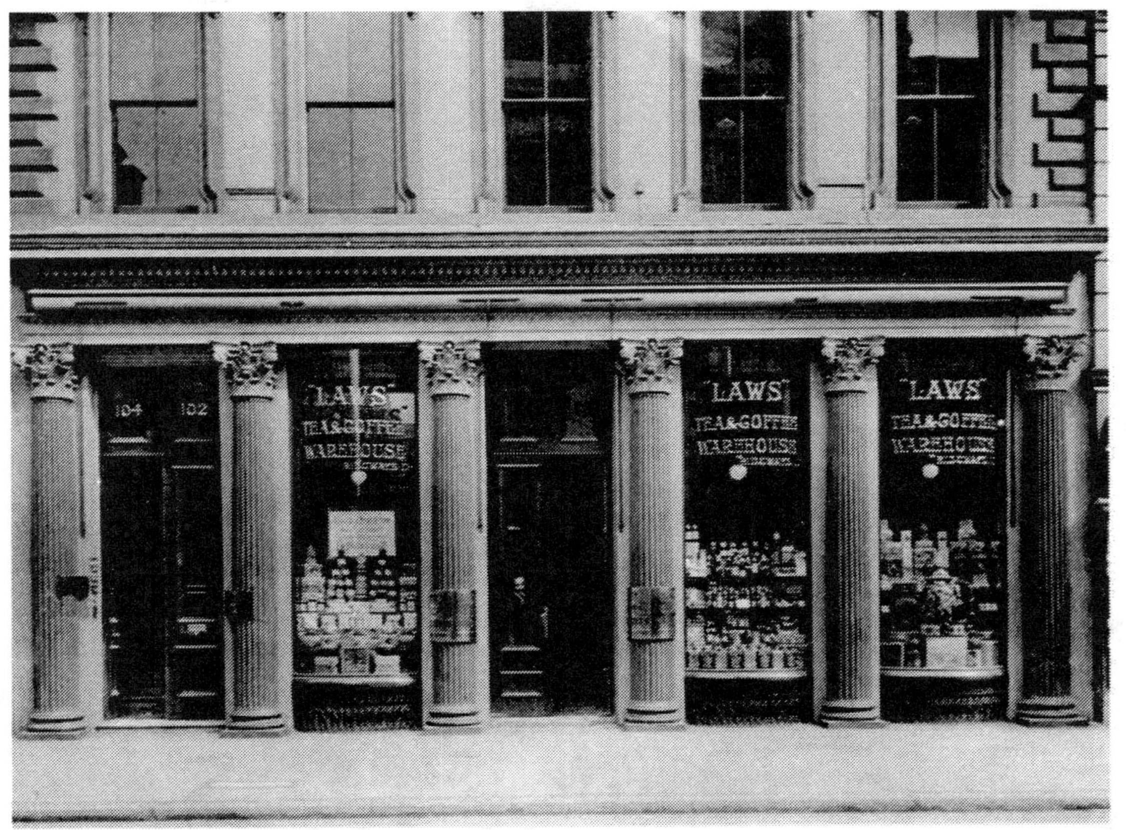

NO. 102, NEW OXFORD STREET, LONDON.

CHAPTER II.

THE ARCHITECTURE OF THE MODERN SHOP-FRONT.

HAVING briefly reviewed the shop-front of a past age, it is interesting and indeed vastly important to turn to a consideration of the complex problem that is presented, when attempting to deal with the shop-front of to-day.

It should be, perhaps, unnecessary to emphasize that a sufficient recognition of the great importance of this problem is the first essential to a systematic review. Necessarily, there are to-day, practical and commercial limitations of the creative faculties which were not imposed upon the designers of the various charming old eighteenth century fronts. The whole character of the distributive industries of the country has changed. Whereas the shop-keeper of the previous generation was contented to rely upon a solidly built reputation as a sufficient advertisement, the shop-keeper of to-day, buffeted by an abnormally developed competition, has so to adapt himself to the needs of his times as to seek a more pronounced advertisement than a good honest reputation.

He sees in his shop-front a happy medium for a properly expressed and unique advertisement. The rapid developments of a revived building trade are at hand to help him. The glass industry has made tremendous progress. He is able to procure sheet and plate glass in large sizes. The manufacture of the rolled steel-joist has been revolutionized. He is relieved of the necessity of a limited opening for his front. Therefore his shop-front becomes the most important part of his premises. It is the permanent and daily advertisement which is to stimulate and encourage the sale of his goods and commodities. Hence it becomes, as the result of a purposeless exaggeration, the aggressively ugly and the unnecessarily prominent features of a disturbed and reasonless street architecture. Throughout all ages true architecture and style—not imitative—have been the result of a logical and proper use of the materials and conditions of work and labour which existed at the time. It is even so to-day. The influence of local materials and requirements mark all great and revolutionary changes in architectural diction and style. But now, at the beginning of a new century, English architects, somewhat behind their brethren in America and on the Continent, are reluctantly compelled to see the vast importance which steel construction must have upon the buildings and the architecture of those buildings, in the near future. Iron, concrete, glass—these are some of the materials to hand. Consequently, these and similar materials should be used for buildings, and even in a limited way for the recreation of the shop-front. That French architects in general and Viollet le Duc in particular realised this fact, is proved by a reference to the latter's "Lectures on Architecture."

The high value of land in London and other large cities demand that buildings shall be many storied. The result is the steel frame building which, as things go at present, is falsely covered with stone or brick; this having no constructional relationship with the carcase. Viollet le Duc, who evidently has half-timber work in his mind, endeavours to show the construction with bold honesty. The iron framework, even as in the old timber structures, is left uncovered, the filling between being in tiles or some other material suitable to the purpose. The upper portion of the building projects out over the lower portion and has, even as in the old Elizabethan timber houses, a depreciating effect upon the real lightness of the actual shop-front.

It is worthy of notice that American architects have made a considerable number of experiments in this connection, shop-front and superstructure being entirely carried out in steel and iron. How they contend with the dangerous difficulties presented by the need of efficiently protecting this metal-work from fire and weather, is not clearly shown. To them at least, the problem of a logical connection between shop-front and superstructure is sufficiently solved by a proper and natural use of similar materials for the whole of the building; for they know that new effects of this discription must necessarily be judged by different canons of taste and discrimination.

The Recessed Shop-Front.

From a consideration of the inherent possibilities of exposed iron construction in direct regard to shop-front designing, notice must be given to an expediency very much adopted at the present time. This is the setting back of the shop-front some two, three or more feet from the actual building frontage instead of making it flush or nearly flush with the plane line of the building overhead. This has many advantages, and the break in the plane has the useful effect of making less apparent the solecism of a heavy building seemingly resting upon a sheet of glass. Besides this, it creates a standing space where an intending customer can quietly admire whatever goods the window may offer for his inspection without being jostled by hurrying and inconsiderate people on the pavement. The idea offers many possibilities of development. The sides of the lobby or loggia can be occupied by show-cases, while in some examples an additional show-case is placed in the centre (Plate xiv). This has the good effect of dividing the crowd and making the inspection of goods easy and perfect by the creation of a circuit. The ceiling and floor of a recessed front give an opportunity of introducing some interesting detail, while the frame itself can be bowed or shaped or planned as desired. There is, however, one disadvantage. In premises absolutely dependent upon the light obtainable from the shop window, the recessing of that window, with a consequent darkening of the shop interior, becomes inadmissible. Considering this setting back from the point of view of its relation with the building over, an elevation is presented with solids slightly relieved, resting upon one huge void, and not, as is usual, resting on a framework of wood and glass. This it seems, because of its honesty, is an improvement, and if the frontage be not too great, it should be easy so to adjust things as to avoid any incongruity of treatment. The use of the sham arch is to be deprecated, for the only natural treatment of a shop-front opening is a square treatment or beam and post.

There is a sound ornamental principle to be deduced from the effect gained by the setting in of the shop-front. The planes of the building surfaces must be broken up with relation to the shop-

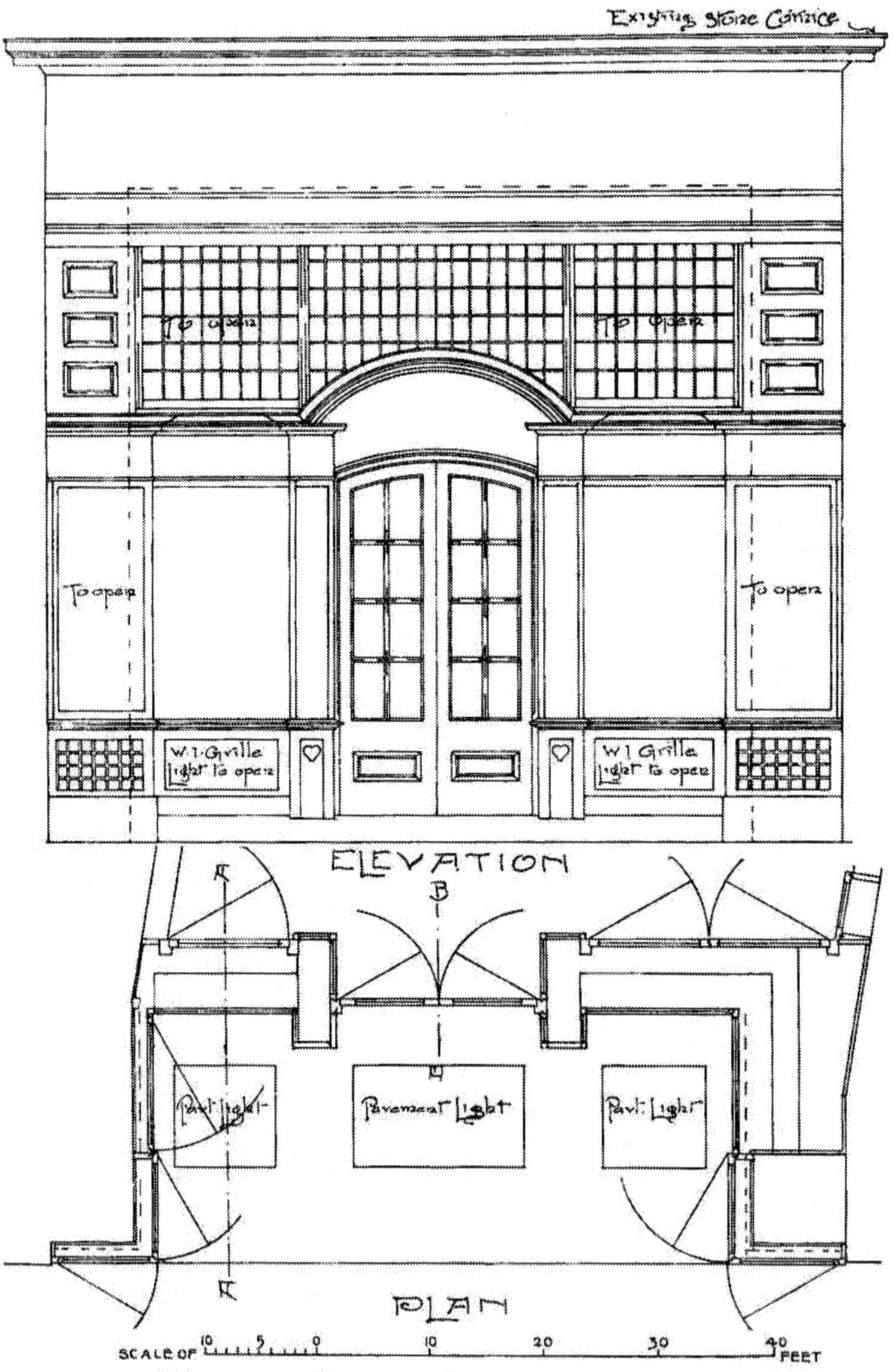

Fig. 14. NO. 65, ST. PAUL'S CHURCHYARD, LONDON.

W. Ernest Hazell, Architect.

front, *i.e.* if this relationship is to be cognate and architecturally recognizable. For instance, the use of bays projecting out over the shop-front below (Plate xv) helps this intention, while the slight

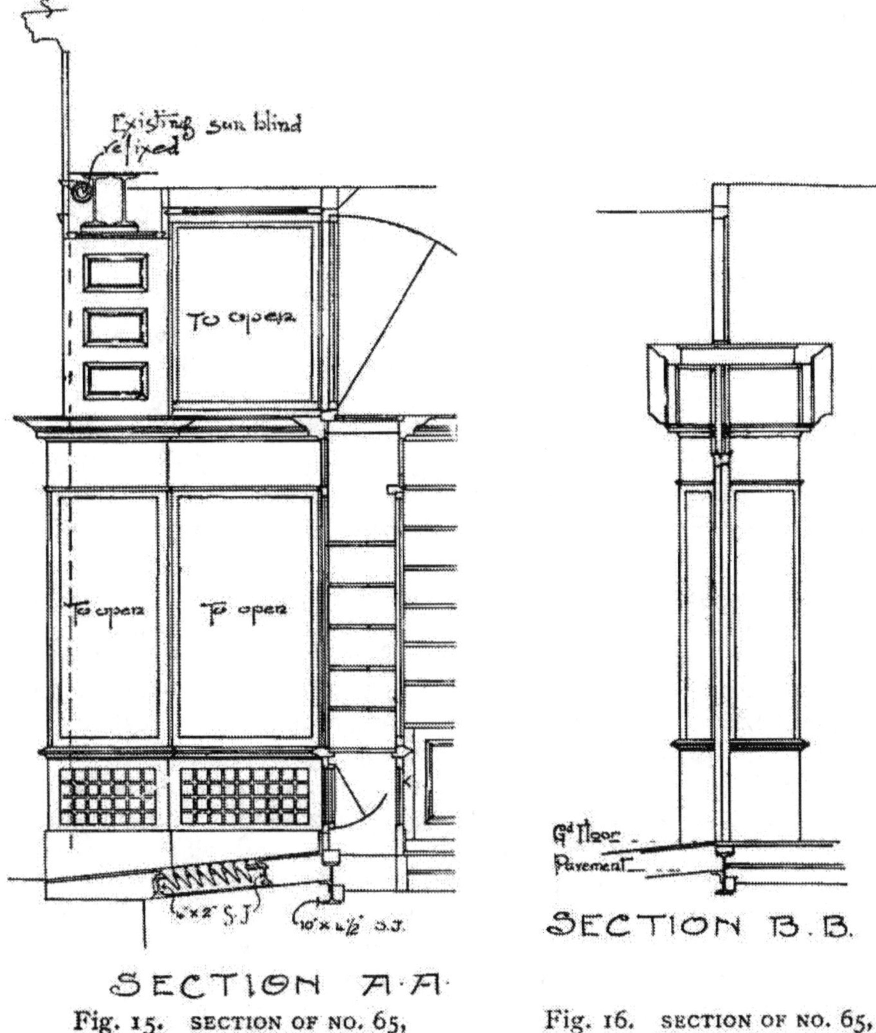

Fig. 15. SECTION OF NO. 65, ST. PAUL'S CHURCHYARD, LONDON.

Fig. 16. SECTION OF NO. 65, ST. PAUL'S CHURCHYARD, LONDON.

curvature of the front itself, as long as it does not distort the lines of perspective, has a not unpleasing effect.

Plate xvi is a typical example and an excellent one to wit, of the modern recessed shop-front. A large amount of display space is allowed for, while the vestibule provides a suitable area wherein the customer is able to quietly and leisurely examine the goods which may be displayed in window and show case. The piers at either side supporting the square-headed entablature look sufficiently strong for their purpose, and although bulky, the shallow showcase, built around the lower portion, duly compensates for the room lost by their comparatively large size. Figures 14, 15, and 16, show the construction and general arrangement of this front.

In Plate xvii the shop-front is recessed some few feet, and has two cleverly introduced triangular bays. The height of effective display is very properly limited by a broad shelf. Above this it is noticeable that a recessed and glazed screen is successfully utilized for the purpose of giving light to the actual shop interior. Figure 17 is a reproduction of the working drawings for this design. Further recessed shop-fronts are illustrated by Plates xviii, xix, and xx.

In the shop-fronts just described, the recess in each case has been merely a recess, and little effort has been made to mitigate in any way the extent of the large void thus created at the bottom of the building. This device of setting back the shop-frame has only a negative success, and further effort must be made to realize fully the possibilities of the recess as a means to a more positive end. Further remarks can be better illustrated by an examination of the front illustrated in Plate xxi. This is one of a well known type of front with which most architects are familiar, and, what is more to the point from a shopkeeper's point of view, one which the general public seem to note and comment upon. The example illustrated was especially selected because it presented features extraneous to the other shop-fronts belonging to the same firm. It will be noticed that the shop-frame is recessed some two-and-a-half to three feet, and two Ionic columns of good proportion and design stand forward and support the superstructure. This is surely admirable. The functional purpose of the columns is honest. The piers at either side are suitably strong, and the actual wood framework is subordinated to the first essential of any facade which has a shop-front below, and which would aim to have direct structural and therefore direct architectural relationship with that shop-front. It matters little that the columns, elevationally, appear to cut the front

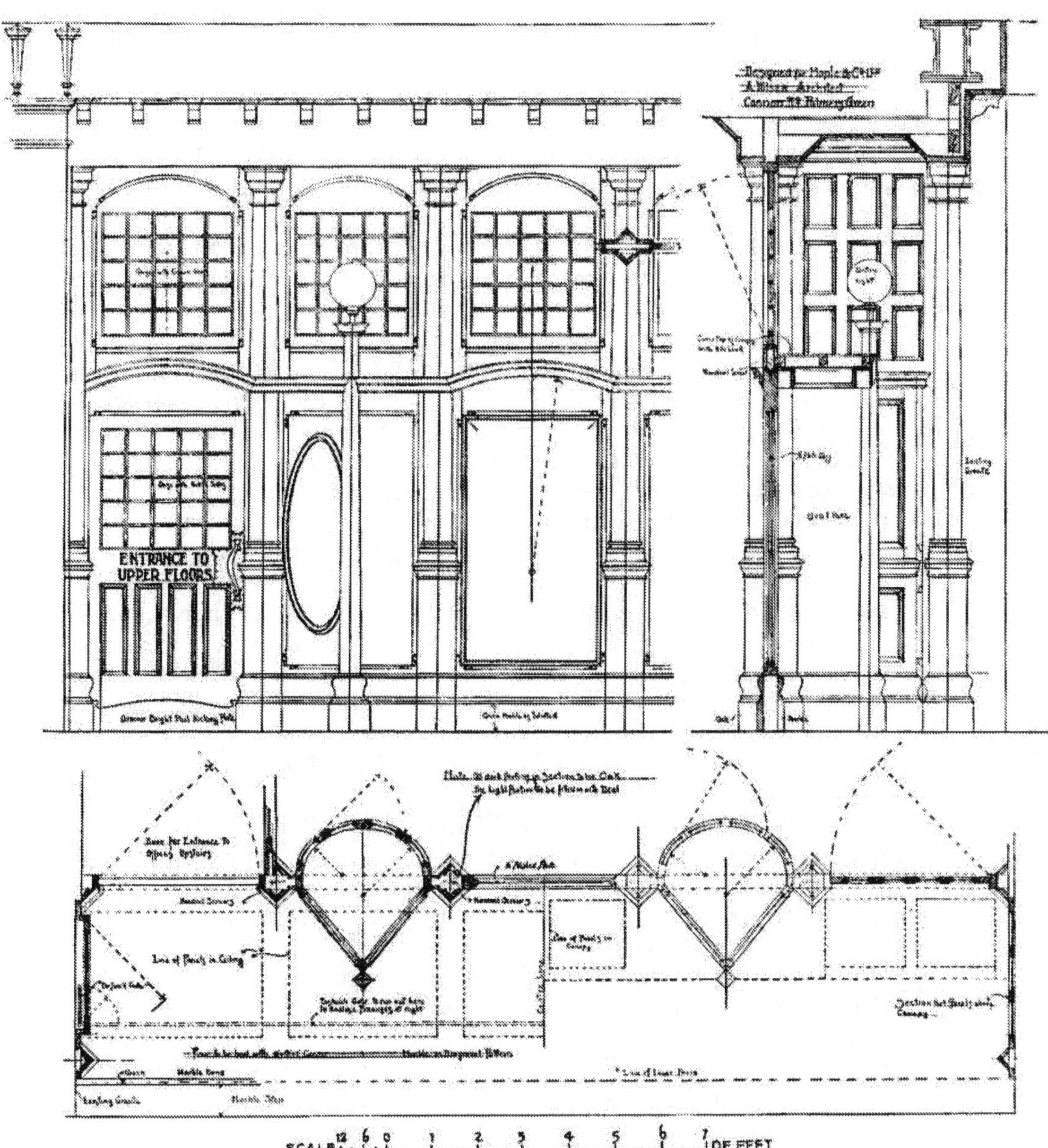

SCALE 12 6 0 1 2 3 4 5 6 7 OF FEET

Fig. 17. NO. 25 CHEAPSIDE, LONDON.

A. Palser, Architect.

into three portions. In reality they do not, and the intending customer, by extending himself or herself about a foot towards the front door, is at once inside the line of the columns and in complete view of the whole window.

Plate xxii is a similar type of front to the last, bold stone columns being used to carry the superstructure.

The shop-front belonging to The Jaeger Wool Co., Glasgow (Plate xxiii), is a recessed front similar in character to the last, and a worthy example of the many shop-fronts of good architectural character which this firm have caused to be erected in many of the principal towns of Great Britain and abroad. The curved vestibule, with its marble paving, is happily conceived and as happily carried out. It provides an abundance of window space for the display of the goods, and at the same time the semi-circular form is conducive to a pleasing and subtle architectural effect. The chief interest of the front, however, lies in the steel supporting columns. Nothing but admiration can be given for the excellent idea of enclosing these with small showcases of octagonal form. Concealed, yet revealed, the support of the building is suitably and usefully indicated. Note, too, how the small glazing bars lend themselves to a pretty symmetrical treatment of window dressing.

There are many interesting fronts but slightly recessed, the frame being set back some one or two feet from the building line and being simply splayed or bowed in the style of the Georgian fronts noticed in the first chapter. The best of these are illustrated by Plates xxiv, xxv and xxvi.

The excellent front which Mr. Edward Howell has had erected for his bookselling business in Liverpool (Plate xxvii) is well worthy of the various encomiums which have been lavished upon it. Without possessing any merit for distinctive detail the design is eminently indicative of the method that should be adopted when it is desirous to obtain in a shop of narrow frontage the maximum amount of display space. In the front under notice the original frontage was only fifteen feet. The new shop-front allowed for an exhibition space of over thirty feet. A glance at the illustration reveals the easy ingenuity which led to this result.

The Type Shop-Front.

Plate xxviii, one of the J. P. Restaurants in London, offers an opportunity for a short digression upon the tendency which large firms are developing for the creation of what, for want of a better term, can be called a type-front. The names of such firms as Messrs. Slaters Limited, Messrs. Lyons and Co., The Maypole Dairy Co., The Sorosis Boot Co., and a host of others instantly recur to the mind in this connection. Such firms as these evolve their special type of shop-front, and this design, altered as required, is made to fit all sorts of positions. Protest must be entered against this cutting and trimming of a design created to the needs of one certain position, but made to fit others for which it was not designed. Possibly there is a desire upon the part of these large monopolies to still further impress a long suffering public with a gorgeous architectural uniformity and sameness; a uniformity, however, usually much too blatantly vulgar, to be ever beauteously sober and tasteful. There is no reason, however (were all the fronts designed in harmony), why they should not be indelibly stamped with certain characteristics of design which would be as much a label for the firm as the most uniform of ugly fronts. The shop-fronts of The Jaeger Wool Co., designed by Mr. Charles E. Dawson, are especially to be commended in this connection.

Plate xxviii, the front already spoken of, is something better than the usual type-front. The two semi-circular bays are pleasant and suggestive of the value of a picturesque perspective, while the glazed frieze over has an artistic as well as a utilitarian purpose.

The International Stores, from Enfield (Plate xxix), is another and very good design for a type-front.

The Projecting Shop-Front.

The next front to be noticed for simplicity's sake has been given the title of the projecting shop-front. The strict enforcement of a uniform code of byelaws has necessarily limited the adoption of this type of front. This seems a pity as it offers for easy realization an architectural and constructional continuity of effect not obtainable by other devices. Under the easy byelaws of earlier times the projecting shop-front was a common and picturesque type, but, now-a-days, with the well ordered inconsiderateness of different authorities the projecting front can scarcely be adopted without setting the whole of the building back in order to provide sufficient ground for the projection of the frames. This would often be prohibitively expensive and in some ways a scarcely justified procedure. When, however, the opportunity naturally occurs, there is a good deal to be said in favour of the objective architectural value to be gained by the adoption of the type. In common with the recessed front its reversion has a dominant negative advantage. There is no assumption of any supporting effect in regard to the building over, the fact of boldly setting the front forward completely dispelling any illusion which might exist in this direction. At the same time it is possible so to treat the front as to give it the inestimable advantage of a partial top-light upon the goods.

Notable for its simple and refined elegance is the front illustrated by Plate xxx, although no top light is arranged for. It is evident that Mr. Cave, the architect, found some inspiration for this design in the old shop-front in the Haymarket. He is to be congratulated upon a clever adaptation of an old method to a modern need.

The Corner Shop.

The corner shop is perhaps the most difficult of all types to deal with in a satisfactory architectural manner, and, because of this it has not been easy to find many suitable illustrations. Generally the corner building is splayed and the shop-front naturally follows the same alignment, two steel columns being placed behind the shop-frame at either corner of the splay. The result from an architectural point of view is more aggravatingly unreal than ever, the corner of the superstructure appearing to have absolutely no support. Consequently in the corner shop more than in the single isolated front, it becomes imperative for the designer to give greater consideration to the treatment of the main angle. The entrance is usually placed at the corner, but it must be pointed out that there is no absolute necessity to do this : in fact, a stronger corner can be made when the entrance is placed in one of the sides.

In a building recently erected at Manchester, two sturdy stone columns, which looked, and actually were, strong enough to support the building over, were placed at each angle of an ordinary splayed corner. The shop-frame was set back some few feet behind and the general effect was entirely good; for the columns, while giving some idea of support to the general elevation, were at the same time quite unobjectionable in so far as any interference with the display of goods were concerned.

Plate xxxi is undoubtedly one of the best planned shop-fronts included in this review, and at the same time it does all that is necessary to indicate how effective and interesting a corner shop can be made. The needs of the business are provided for in a remarkedly clever fashion. For instance, the small window upon the left side of the picture is made to open, this portion being used for the purposes of a second-hand bookstall. The stall-board is kept high and the space underneath is used for the display sheets of the daily newspapers. The main windows on the right are recessed 1ft. 6ins., a convenient standing place being thus created. The steel supporting columns at each corner of the vestibule have small show-cases formed around them, the three openings to the entrance being 4ft. 6ins. wide. The bookstall proper, a window 6ft. wide, made to open, is upon the left side of the vestibule. The door with side lights is 6ft. over all.

The Double-Storied Shop-Front

In a review necessarily concise, it is to be regretted that more space cannot be devoted to a consideration of the double-storied shop-front, an essentially modern evolution representative of the commercial progressiveness of the times. This sort of shop-front is becoming more largely adopted every day, more especially by carriage dealers, furniture warehousemen, and sellers of a similar class of goods. The idea seems a natural adoption of the *entresol* arch, the latter being an expedient adopted some years ago for the purpose of giving some idea of support for the upper parts of a shop-fronted building. For some unknown reason this device fell into disfavour. More recently it has been revived, the acute shopkeeper seeing that by such means he will be enabled to enlarge an already large exhibition space by having a second or mezzanine floor to his shop-front. The arch springing from the first floor level, whether elliptical or semi-circular, has necessarily a large glass tympanum which gives abundant light to the mezzanine floor, and at the same time, the window thus formed can be used for the display of suitable goods. These can be seen from the further side of the street and can, obviously enough, be made sufficiently attractive to catch the eye of the casual pedestrian, or to interest the passing omnibus traveller. The result from an architectural point of view, can, in the case of the single or isolated front, scarcely be given unqualified praise. The need of still providing a large and wide ground floor window space does not allow for adequate abutments at either side, the concealed girder being more often than not brought into use as a tie. On the other hand if the *entresol* arch be honestly constructional it must perforce make unfair use of such abutments as may be afforded by the buildings on either side. Assuming the usual street architecture these side buildings are more often than not shops, and consequently useless as abutments for a possible arch with its powerful thrusts. Hence the adoption of the rolled steel joist and a loss of architectural truth by the useless creation of a sham arch. Indeed the use of the *entresol* arch when applied to the single isolated front does not seem to be architecturally helpful. This treatment however, when used in connection with shops in series becomes more satisfactory. The continuance of the arches in successful constructional repetition is strengthening in effect, both as to the shop-fronts themselves, and also upon the architectural whole of the building.

Of the double-storied front with *entresol* arch an excellent example is to be found in the new premises built for Messrs. Debenham and Freebody, in London (Plate xxxii). Sincere congratulations must be offered the architects upon the production of this admirable modern building, a building whose interests are, perhaps, for the reasons of this book, chiefly centred in the shop-fronts. The general adoption of Carrara ware for the most recently erected business premises was followed in this case with much resulting crispness of effect, the defining lines being cleverly and suitably marked with the characteristic ornamentation which is easy to the material. It will be noticed that the end and entrance shop has a central door, the windows being splayed back upon either side with a certain amount of effect. It could also have been completely recessed or otherwise planned to taste. Many other pleasing diversities of form are encouraged by the latent possibilities of the treatment, and much dressy and interesting detail might be added. For the designer, having first established direct structural relationship with the superstructure, is thus released to a pleasant freedom in regard to the treatment of the actual shop-frame itself.

From a consideration of the *entresol* arch as a governing factor in shop-front designing attention must be given to another type of double-storied front; the front where the upper storey is not limited by a real or apparent arch but is treated more or less purely as a square-headed opening. Before doing this, however, notice must be taken of the small dairy shop in New Cavendish Street, London (Plate xxxiii). This front is distinctive because it is a case, and a good case, where the superstructure is really structurally dependent upon the real arch which spans the shop-front opening. It is a good opportunity of doing the right thing which has unerringly been taken advantage of by the architect. Consequently there is much pleasure to be gained in giving the design, in spite of a little too obvious originality in the details, almost unstinted praise. The design has a self-contained success which is all its own. The hood over the arch gives depth and strength while the bowed oriels come quite happily over the abundance of solids which mass and give character to the work upon either side of the shop opening.

Plate xxxiv is an excellent and scholarly design of the square-headed double-storied shop-front. It satisfactorily demonstrates that, by the enlarging of the glass voids of the lower portion, a chance is offered for making better proportional adjustments between the lower and upper portions of the concerned building. Noticeable in regard to this front are the granite pilasters between the windows, which are carried up as vertical balancing lines through the whole height of the building. A small indication is given in the illustration of the clever manner in which the space between these pilasters is filled with large bays. Thus there are no heavy superimposed solids, and both the building and the shop are one architectural whole.

A commentary upon the double-storied shop-front must include reference to such a front as that illustrated by Plate xxxv. This front, it will be observed, is as regards actual display space limited to some seven or eight feet from the ground, the space above this being utilised either as mezzanine story, or else it becomes a low ceiled balcony or gallery which extends completely around the inside of the shop. Access to this can, and is often, gained by means of a small spiral staircase from the back of the shop. The gallery can be usefully employed as a store or even as an additional show place for the shop interior. In this front, as in that at Hanover Square, London, there is much clever decoration. Especially admirable is the graceful delicacy of the characteristic French detail.

Reverting to Plate xxii, the mezzanine floor idea has also been adopted here for the purpose of gaining additional artistic and useful elevation of all the parts.

It is worthy of mention that the requirements of the London Building Act insist that "no part of the woodwork of any shop-front shall be fixed higher than twenty-five feet above the level of the pavement of the public footpath in front of the shop." This prohibition would, of course, govern very largely the designing of double-storied shop-fronts in the Metropolis. Special cases, however, requiring greater height than allowed by this clause would be always given further consideration by the authorities.

The Shop-Front in Series.

Having given a short review of some of the more modern shop-front designs, a few remarks might still profitably be added anent the larger issues of the problem, more especially with respect to a satisfactory solution of how to design a series of shop-fronts as parts of one large architectural whole. Mention has already been made of the possibilities of the *entresol* arch in this direction, and from that idea further attention should be given to the method adopted in regard to the lower portions of the new Ritz Hotel, Piccadilly, London. Here the whole of the main building has been brought out over the pavement, and is boldly carried upon a granite arcading sufficiently bulky to be amply satisfying as to its powers of support, the actual shop-frame being set back behind. The architectural value of this idea, so largely adopted in Paris and other large continental cities, is very obvious. A real support for the building is obtained without the aid of concealed girder work. No flagrant deviation from the laws of traditional proportions are made. The building, may it be said, is treated rationally, and there is no need to give consideration to the possibilities of dealing with the modern problem by the creating of a new and untried code of proportioning. The shop-frame itself is set back and can be treated in various ways. A sun-blind is not necessary while a covered walking space is provided, where, sheltered from weather,

Plate 14.

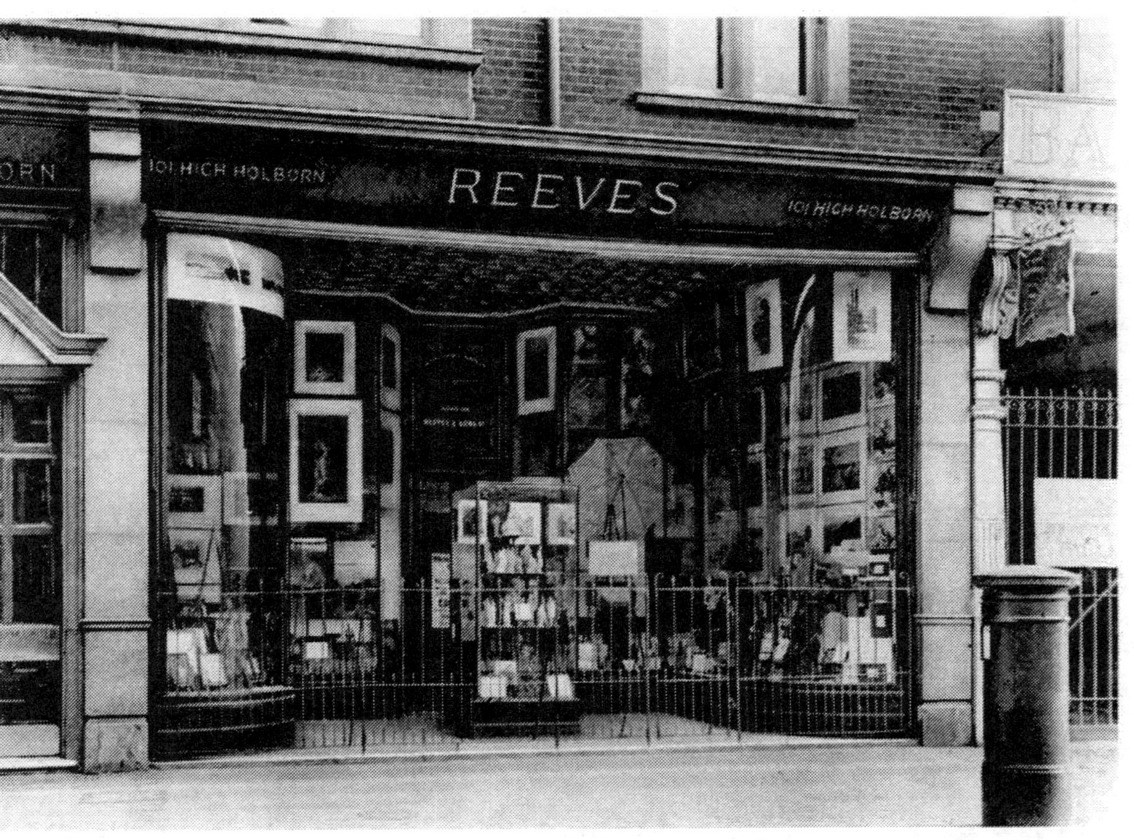

NO. 101, HIGH HOLBORN, LONDON.

Plate 15.

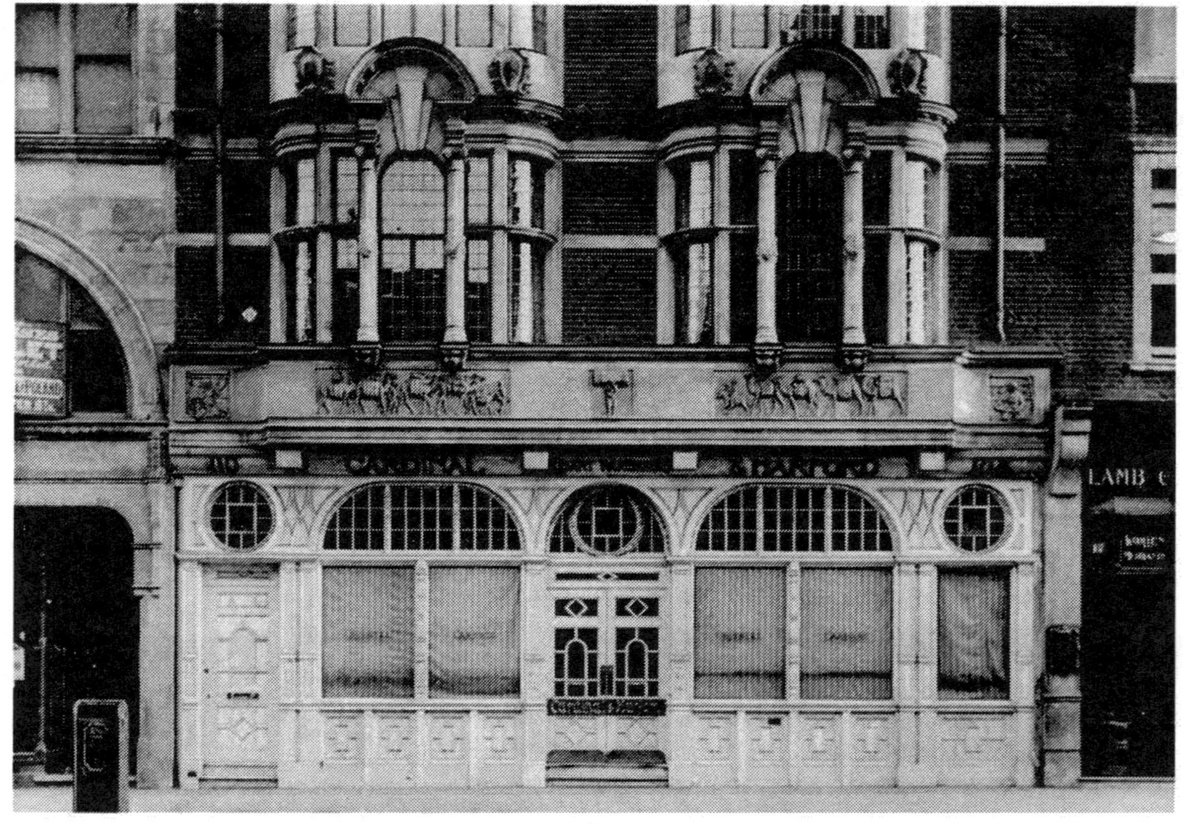

NOS 108 & 110, HIGH HOLBORN, LONDON.

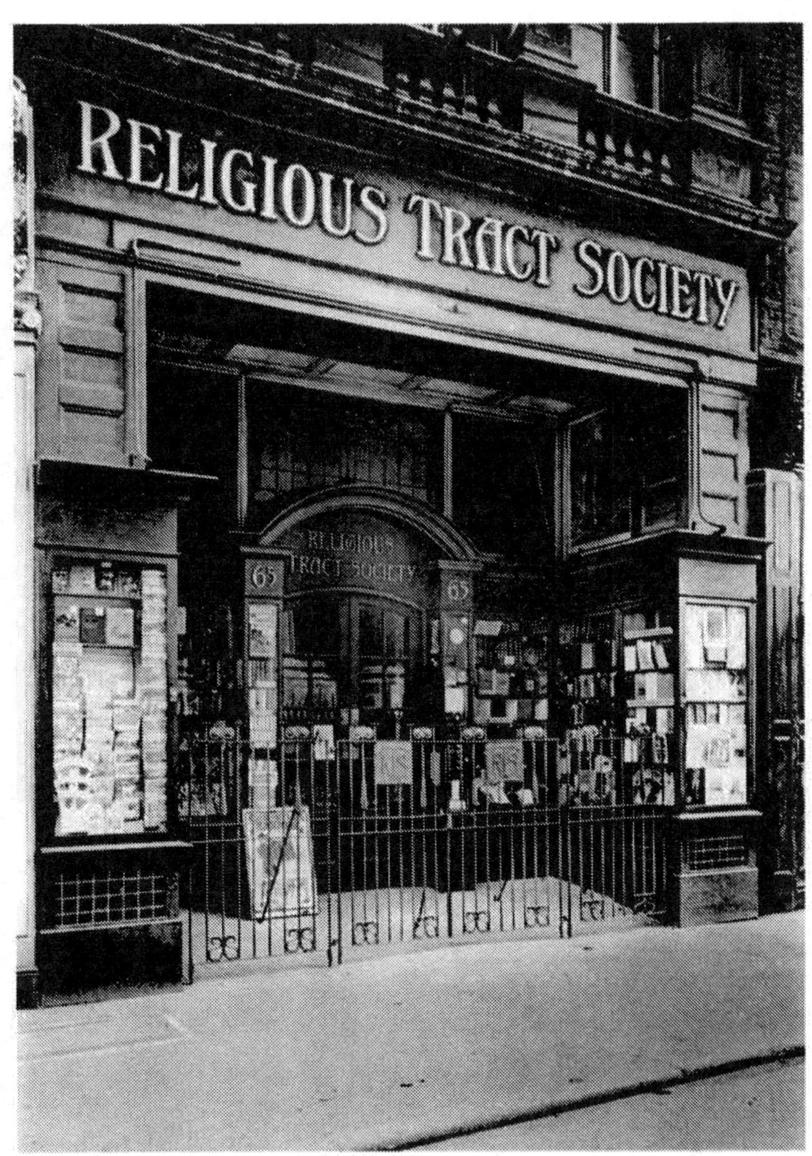

NO. 65, S. PAUL'S CHURCHYARD, LONDON.

Plate 17.

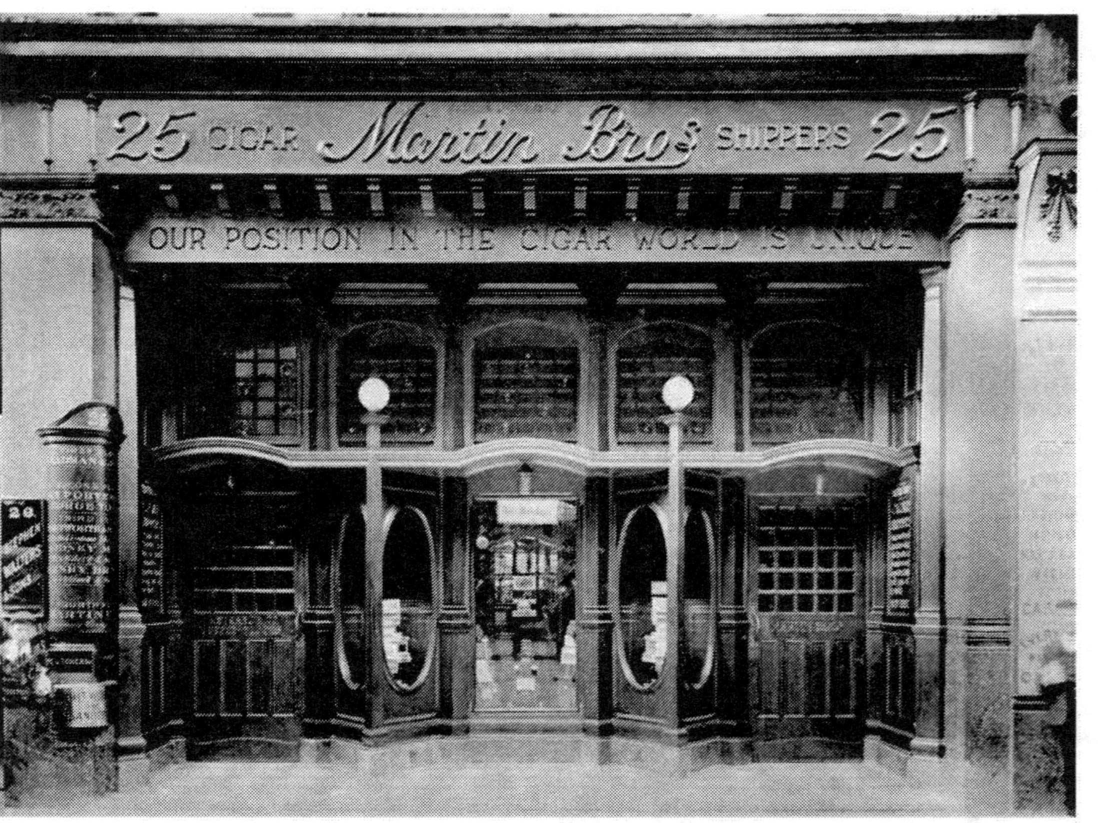

NO. 25, CHEAPSIDE, LONDON.

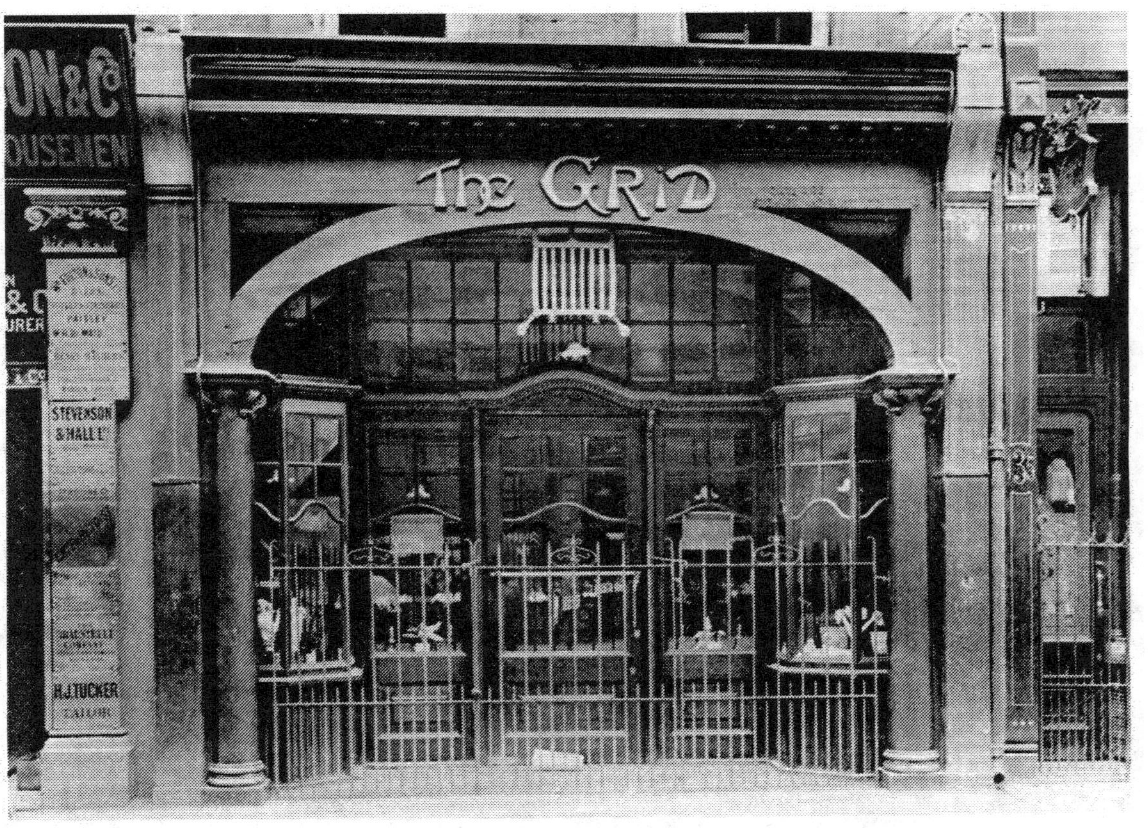

NO. 136, CHEAPSIDE, LONDON.

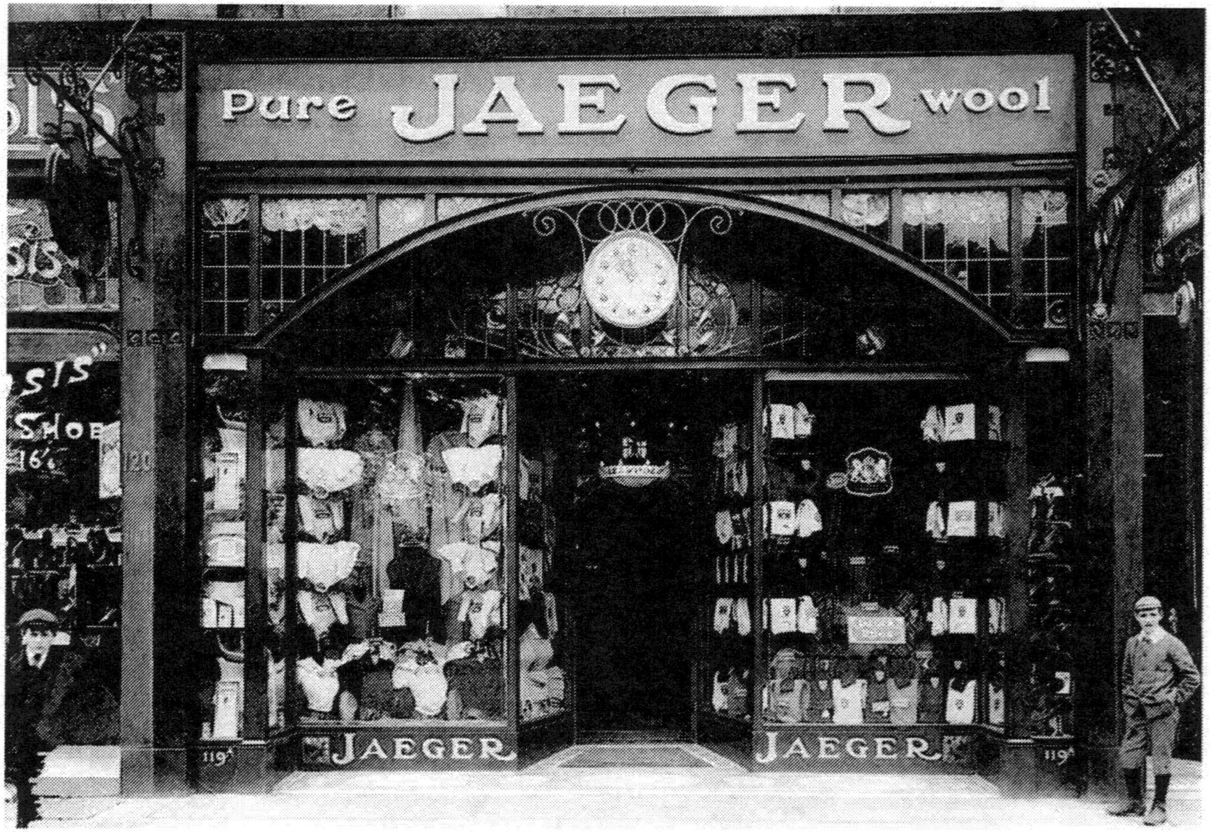

Plate 19.

NO 119A, PRINCES STREET, EDINBURGH.

Plate 20.

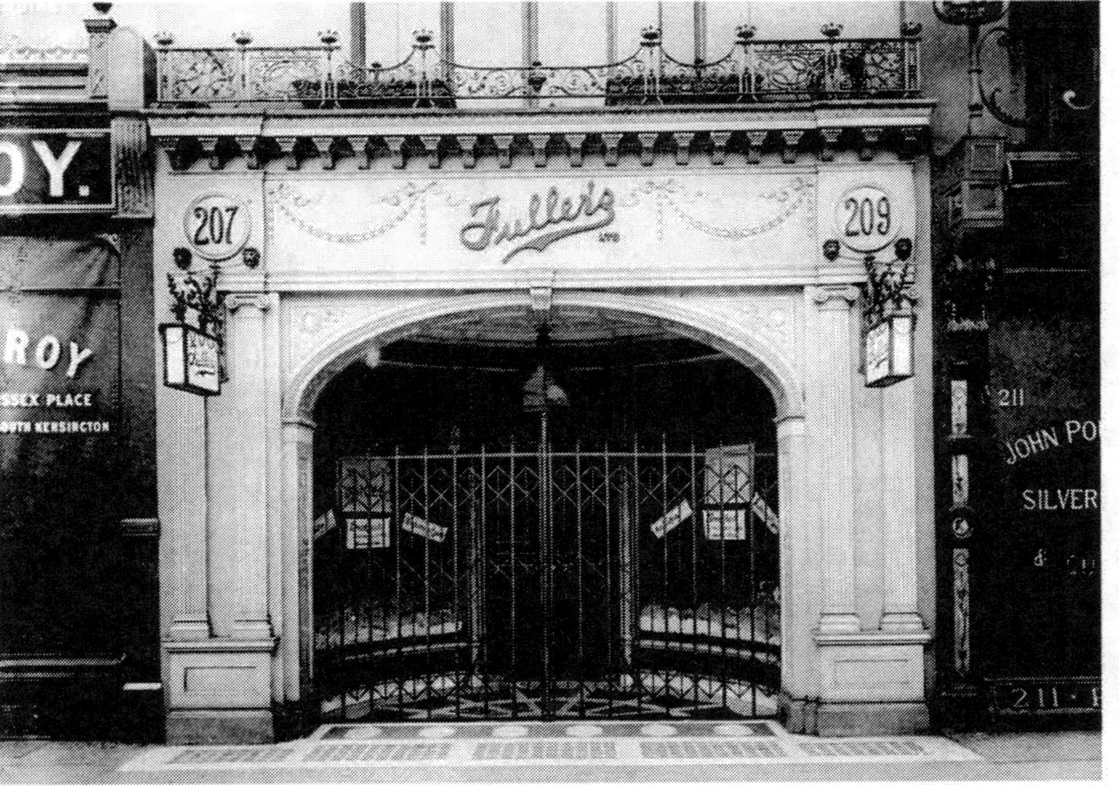

NO. 209, REGENT STREET, LONDON.

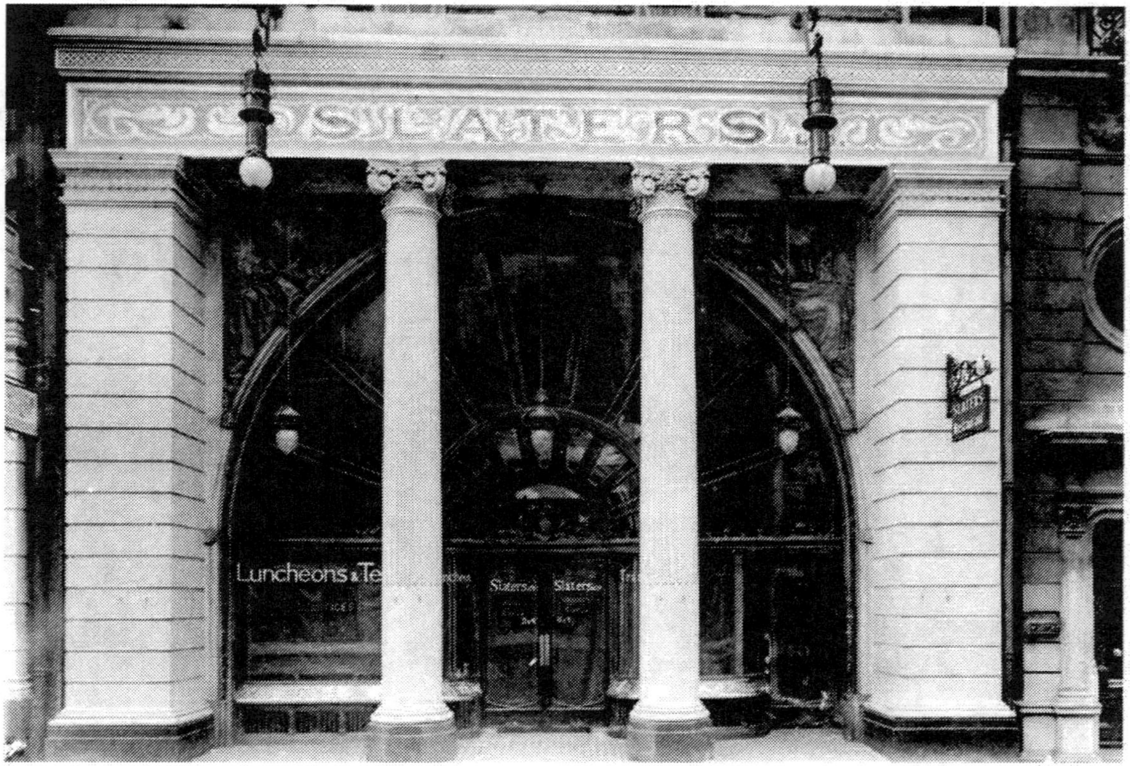

NO. 212, PICCADILLY, LONDON.

Plate 22.

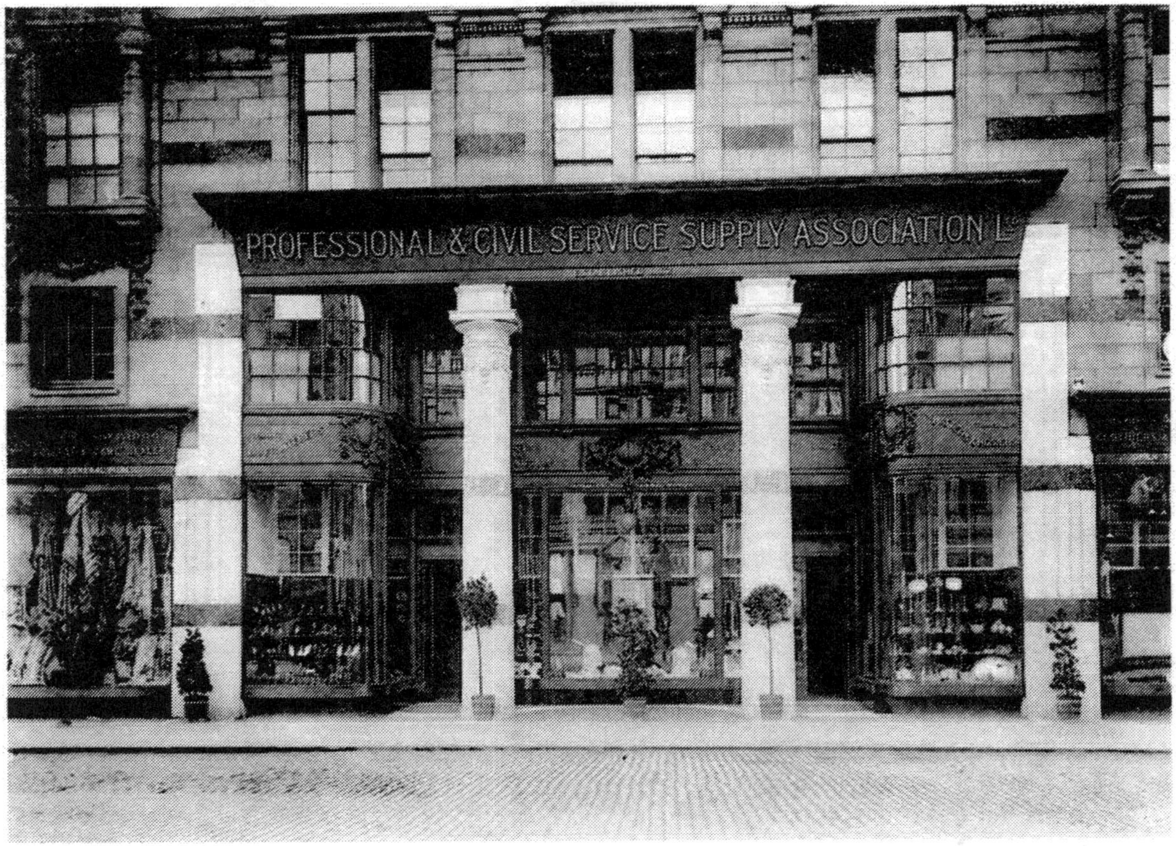

NO. 80, GEORGE STREET, EDINBURGH.

Plate 23.

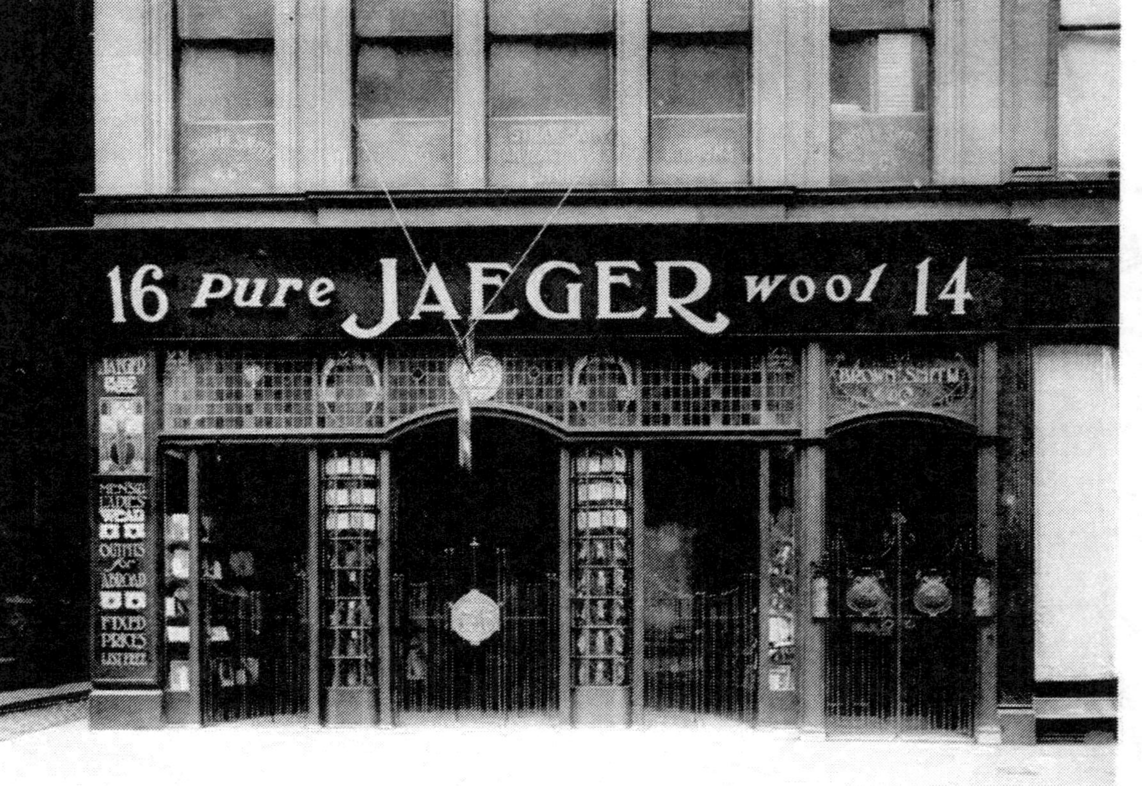

NO. 16, BUCHANAN STREET, GLASGOW.

Plate 24.

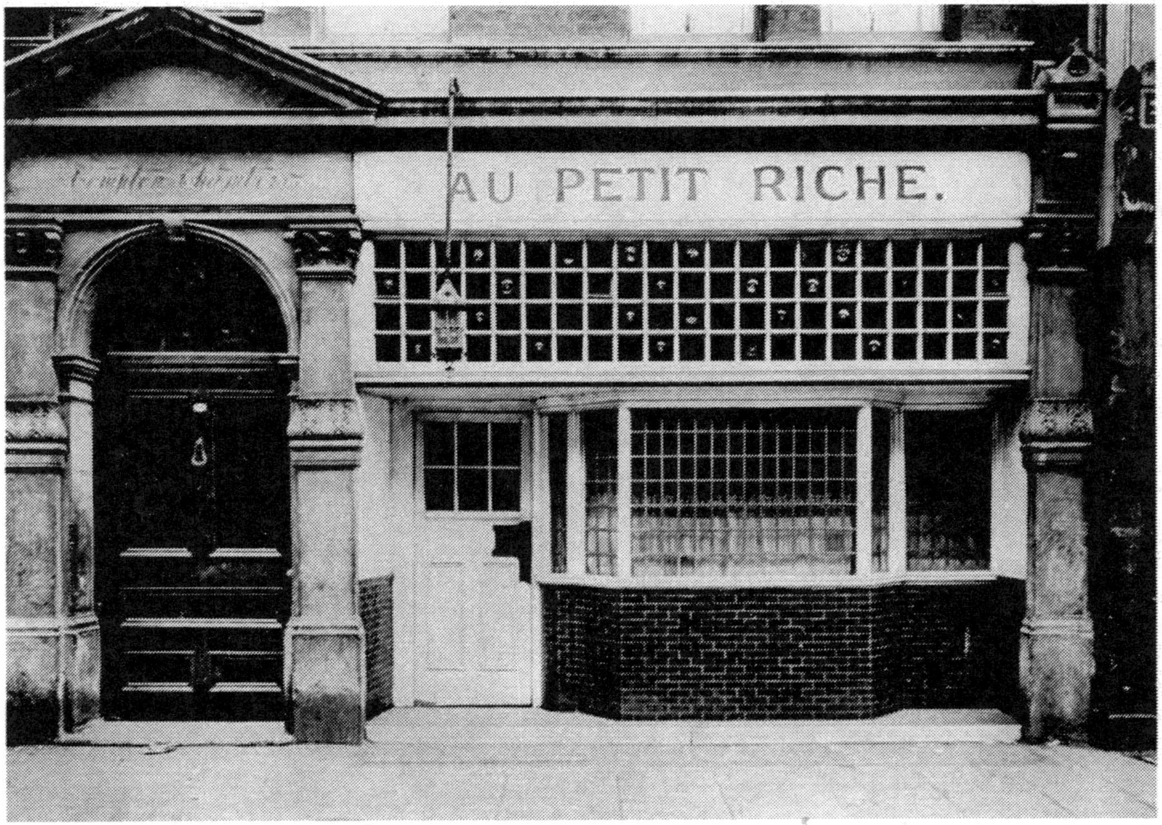

NO. 44, OLD COMPTON STREET, LONDON.

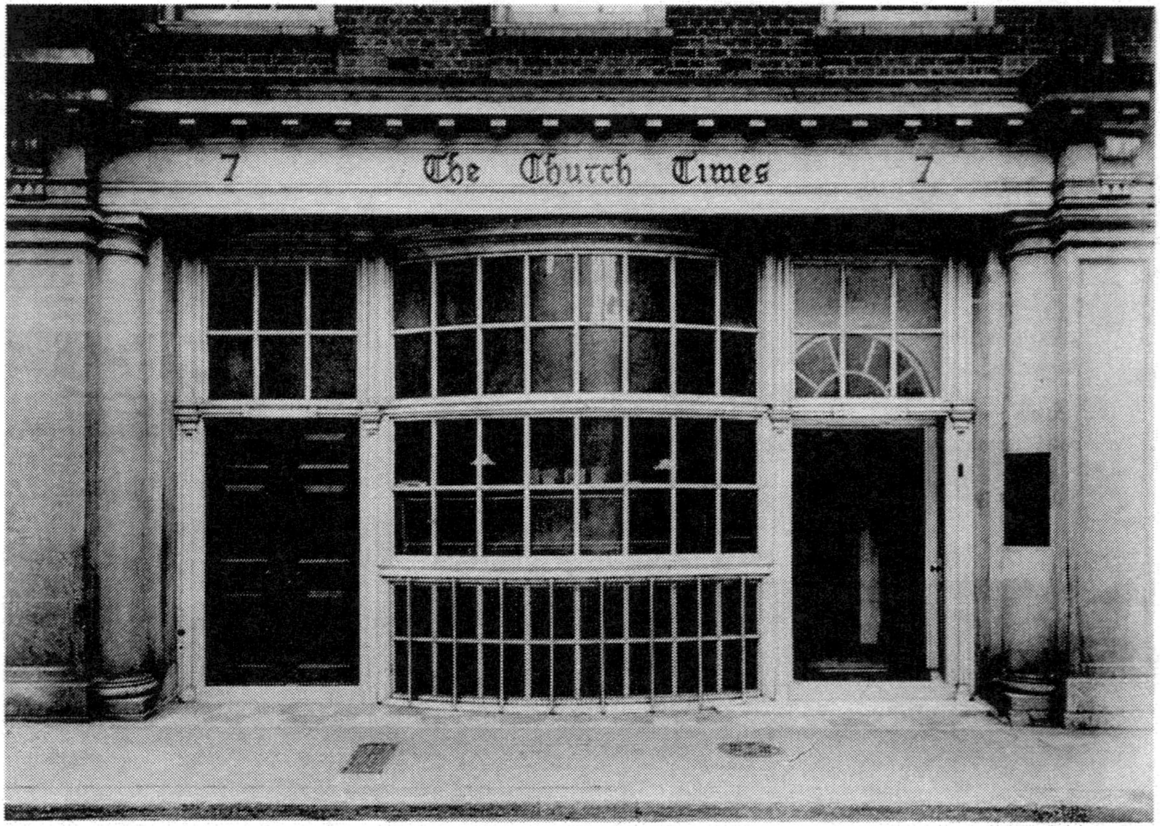

NO. 7, PORTUGAL STREET, LONDON.

Plate 26.

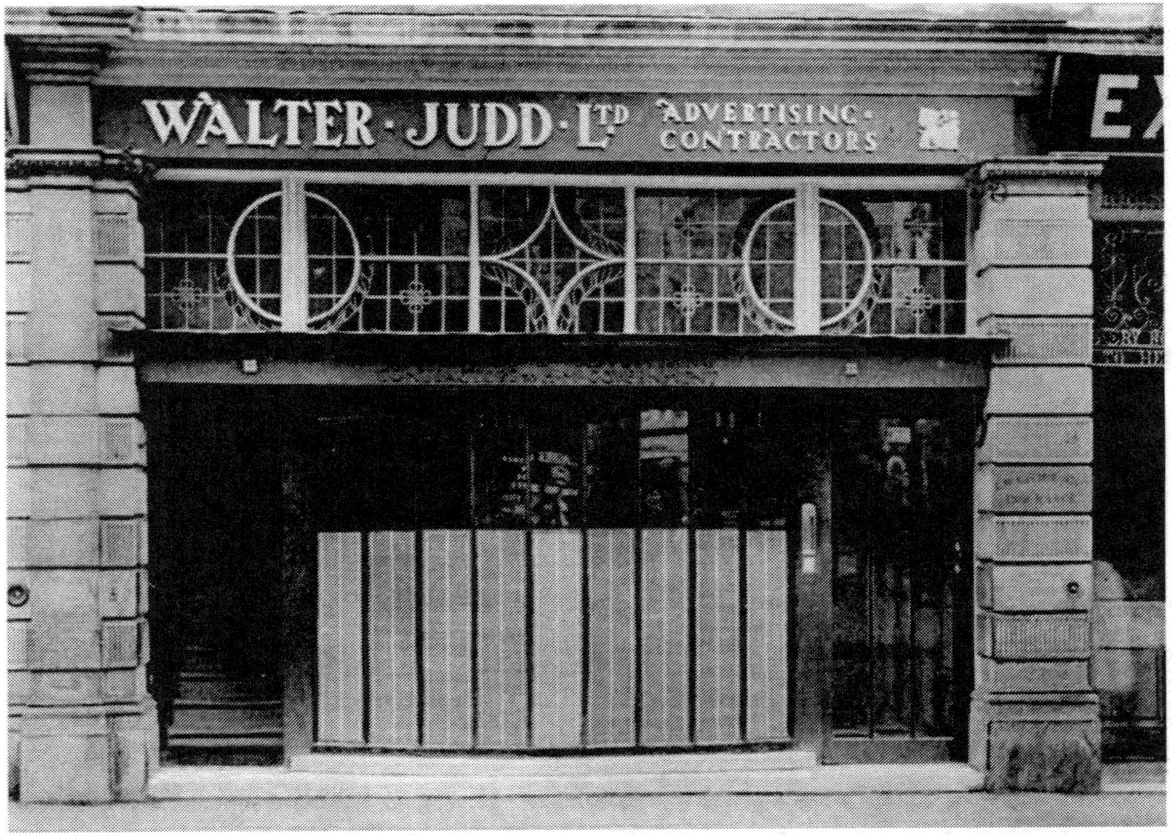

NO. 5. QUEEN VICTORIA STREET, LONDON.

Plate 27.

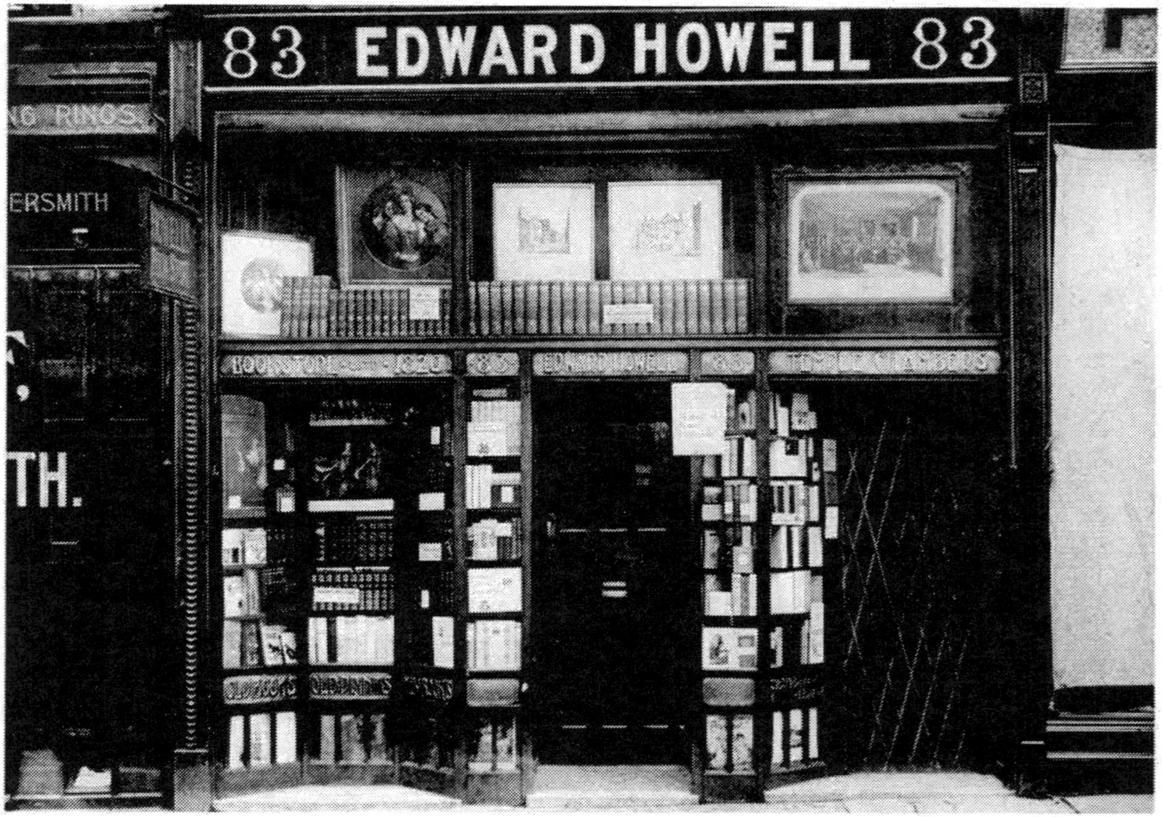

NO. 83, CHURCH STREET, LIVERPOOL.

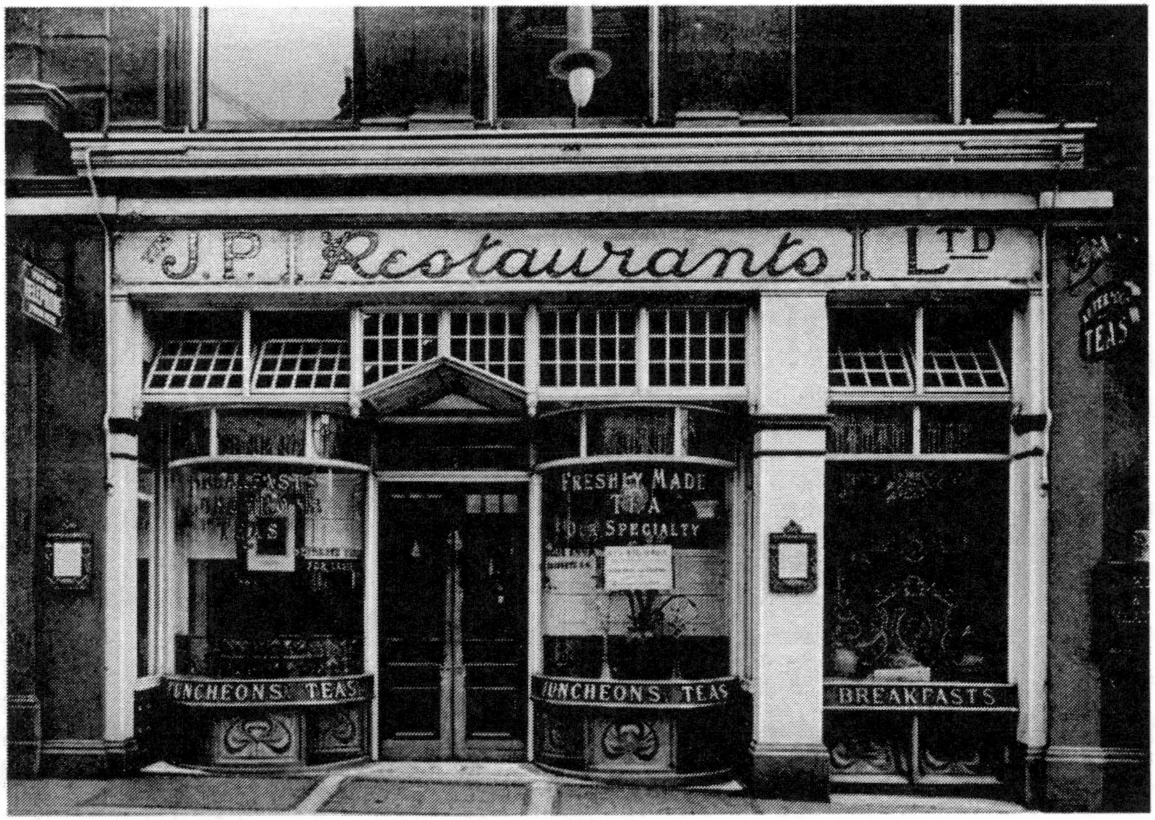

Plate 28.

NO. 17, CHARTERHOUSE STREET, LONDON.

Plate 29.

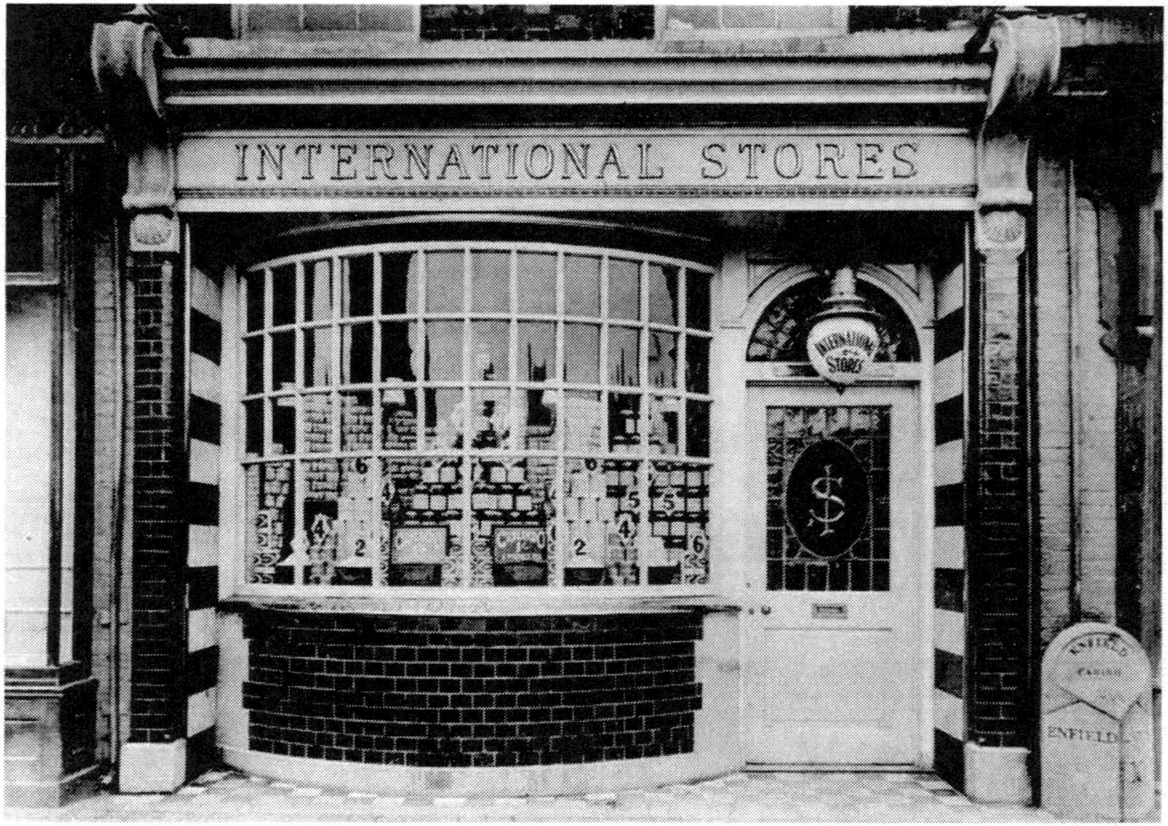

MARKET PLACE, ENFIELD.

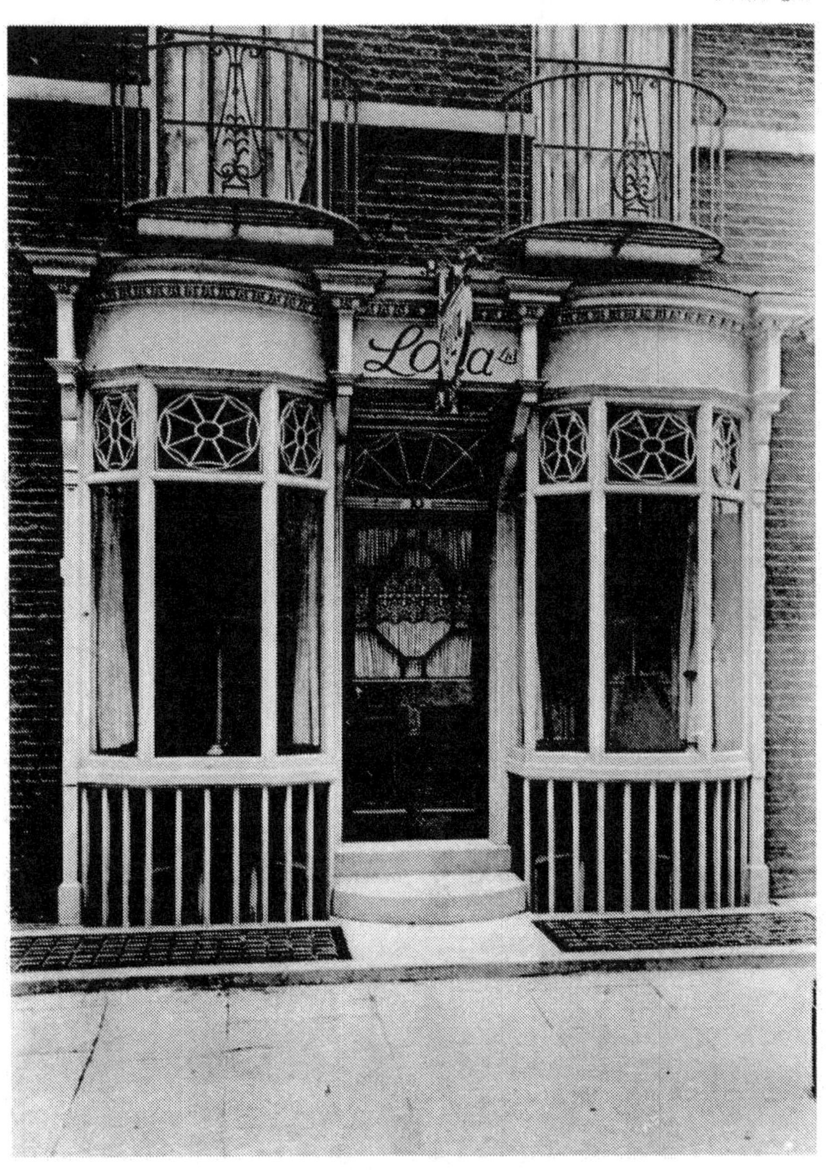

NO. 10, DOVER STREET, LONDON.

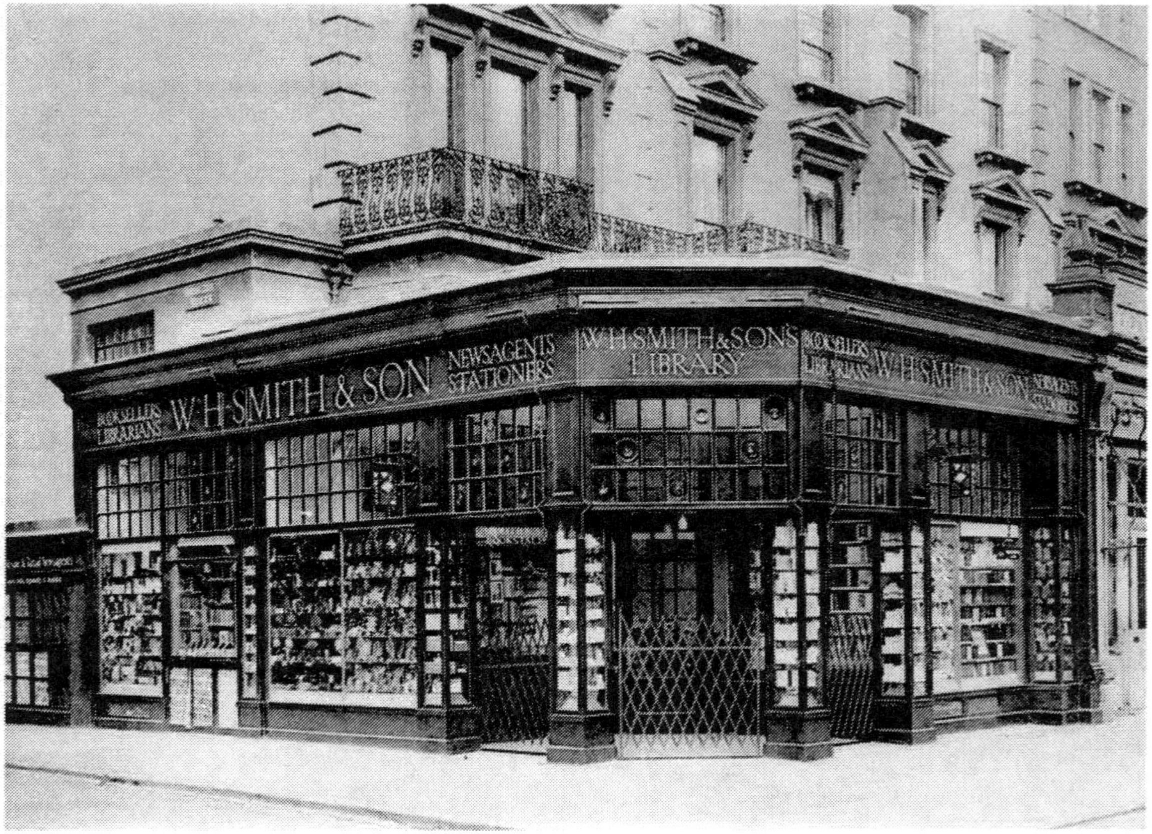

Plate 31.

NO. 103, HIGH ROAD, KILBURN, LONDON.

NOS. 17—37, WIGMORE STREET, LONDON

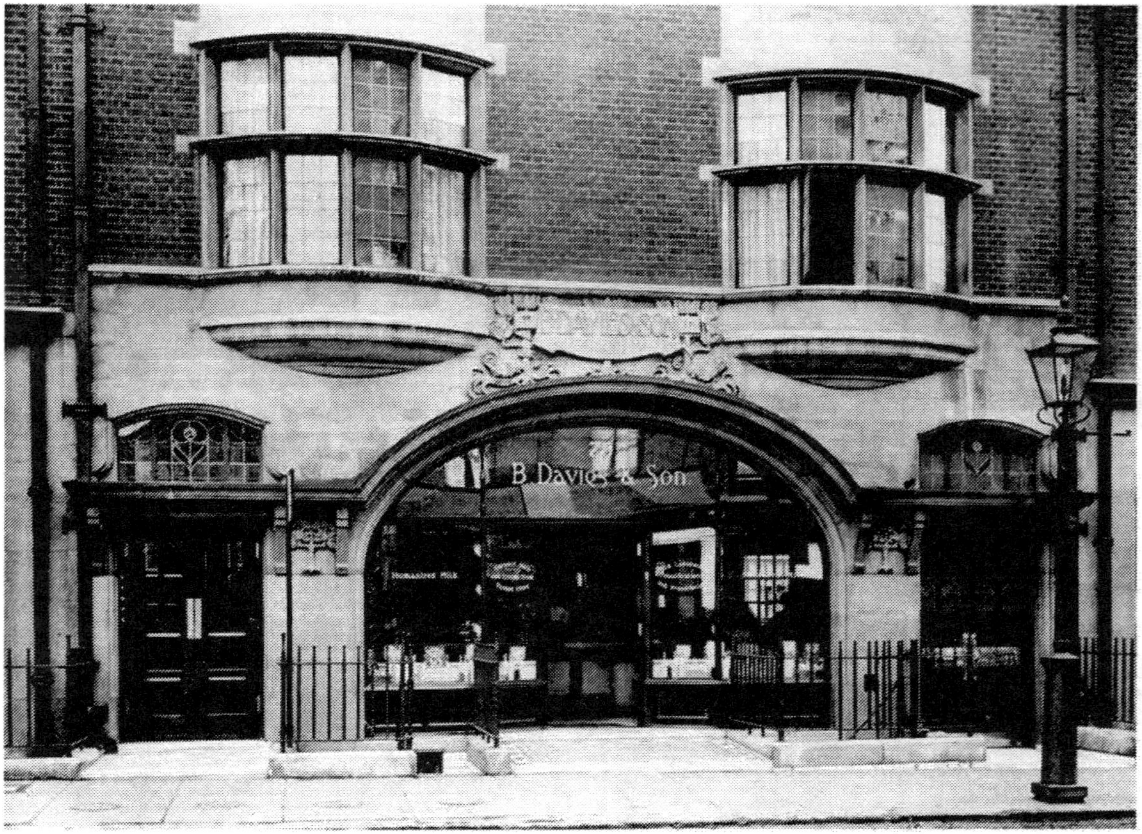

NO. 79, NEW CAVENDISH STREET, MARYLEBONE, LONDON.

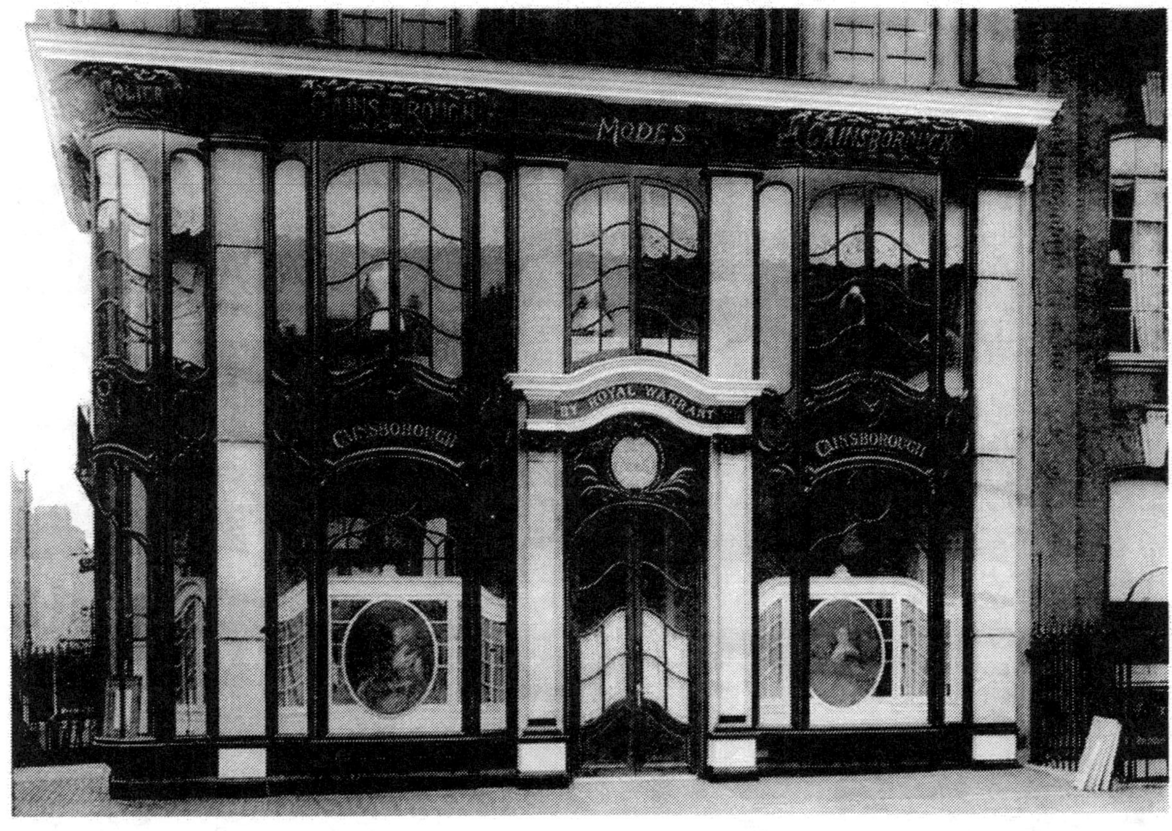

NO. 25, HANOVER SQUARE, LONDON.

NOS. 46, 47, 48, LOMBARD STREET, LONDON.

leisured and comfortable inspection of the goods can take place. It is possible to suggest a further improvement to this and, perhaps, a necessary improvement. Where the byelaws will not allow of the bringing forward of the superstructure, set back the whole of the ground floor shops, letting the colonnade be now at the front of the building line, and not, as at the Ritz Hotel, at the outside of the street pavement. This creates a second or covered shopper's pavement alongside the street or main pavement. Such a double pavement as is suggested would be an inestimable boon in a crowded thoroughfare, there being evolved for the pleasure of the shopper all the comforts and distinct advantages of the single recessed shop-front. In fact this continuous colonnade is the natural development of the recessed front carried, when considered in series, to its logical and obvious conclusion. The loss of light occasioned by the shadowing of piers and arches must be considered in a possible adoption of this idea.

A reference to an illustration of Regent Street before 1848 shows this noble thoroughfare with a colonnade extending the whole of its length. This was done away with because of the great loss of light occasioned by the columns. In suggesting the revival of this old idea for extended thoroughfares of modern shops, it might be pointed out that the difficulty of adequate lighting might be contended with by placing some powerful pavement lights in the flat roof of the colonnade; for the idea apart from the difficulties of light, possesses the same architectural and utilitarian advantages common to the other idea adopted at the Ritz Hotel. It might be desirable to take this gallery or colonnade up two stories, and of adopting the idea contained in the success of the old Chester Rows. An attempt was made in Shaftesbury Avenue, London, to give definite form to such a suggestion. Two stories of shop-fronts with stairs leading from the streets at various intervals were erected upon a triangular site. For some reason or other, the scheme, however, was not a financial success.

It has not been thought necessary to illustrate arcades in this volume as the difficultty of their proper architectural treatment is not great.

CHAPTER III.

THE PRACTICAL REQUIREMENTS OF THE MODERN SHOP-FRONT.

THERE is abundant need for designers to recognise the very necessary adaptation of the shop-front to the needs of the trade or business whose distributive agency it is. The shop-front which might be aptly suitable for a grocer or ironmonger is flagrantly out of place when intended to isolate the distinction of a certain piece of millinery. Indeed, it is largely owing to architects' neglect of this point that the present day shop-front is so terrible, terrible in its sameness, and terrible in the continued desire upon the part of the shop-keeper for the all glass front. While recognising this desideratum when it is applied to a draper's or similar class of shop, the need of an all glass treatment entirely disappears when dealing with the provision of suitable window spaces for a jeweller, or possibly a bookseller. Consequently some remarks might profitably be written as to the type of front which would be most suitable for the needs of various businesses. Noticeable is the practice of the French colour merchant. Invariably the shops devoted to this business are elevationally planned in radial segments, each segment exhibiting a certain colour of the spectroscope. Confessedly the result is somewhat startling, and æsthetically not especially pleasing. At the same time a more clever adaptation of the same idea might easily be made effective and artistic. The introduction of colour into a shop-front design is at all times worthy of recommendation.

Considering how to define, in the design of the front, the nature of the business, difficulties present themselves. Architecturally speaking it would be unwise to ask that such definition should be anything very concrete in character. It should merely be a natural result produced out of an honest attempt to give the front nothing more than sufficient thought in regard to suitability of material, form of plan and a general convenience of working. At the same time, while recognising these more or less abstract principles, they should become no insuperable barrier to the addition of some form of decoration, superfluous in itself, but valuable as forming an artistic accessory, which, like the stone signs of the earlier times, might be an elementary indication of the business carried on.

Two excellent designs illustrate the foregoing remarks. The first (Plate xxxvi), a game and fishdealer's shop, designed by Messrs. Penty and Penty of York, has both those abstract and concrete qualities which are so desirable. A better design for a fishmonger's shop could scarcely be conceived. The whole design is full of purpose and expression, and no hesitancy need be marked in ascribing to it many superlative merits. The admirable modelled and panelled plaster frieze is artistic and interesting. The windows simply contrived for opening and closing and low in their height are surely the best for the limited display of fish and game. Again, notice must be given to, and praise tendered for, the artistic simplicity of the wrought iron-work which comes in front of the stall-board; also for the cleverly detailed carving. In fact, all that is required in this front to tell of name and business is characterized by the front itself in a quiet and telling fashion that is wholly delightful.

The other front (Plate xxxvii), is a modern butcher's shop at Bournemouth carried out in faience by Messrs. Carter and Co., of Poole.

Materials.

In considering the selection of materials for the construction of the shop-front it would be as well to bear strongly in mind what has been written in the foregoing paragraphs. The use and choice of material is largely governed by the same conditions which affect the building of the design according to the varying needs of different trades. There is a tendency, more especially in regard to the opprobrious public house, to design and carry out fronts in faience, or some other vitreous or glazed ware. Special attention is drawn to the Kardomah front, Liverpool, Plate xxxviii. This is carried out in white faience, the numbers, lettering, and small chequered work being in mosaic. The small name plate at the sill level is in copper, the oak doors being also partly covered with the same metal. Though it is exceedingly doubtful if the unbiassed critic would pronounce this front a complete architectural success, yet, at the same time it is admirable for the many good suggestions it offers. Apart from a pleasing solidity in regard to all its parts, it is valuable as an example of the restrained use of colour. The gold mosaic work of the lettering is not out of harmony with the burnished copper on the doors, and is a quiet and subtle relief to the dull monotony of tone given by the white faience. From the shop-keeper's point of view, attractiveness is the quality he mostly demands in the design of his shop-front. He understands the glint of a little gold or the bright attractiveness of a copper covered door. Keeping this in mind it is natural to suggest that the introduction of a little colour, bridled by a complete understanding of its proper limitations, is for the æsthetic betterment of the shop-front. Plate xxi is another example where soberly coloured mosaic is utilised for the purpose of giving life and character to the design. The figures in the mosaic spandrels are cleverly interpreted in the material and have a charming effect.

Contemporary with the introduction of faience for shop-fronts is the use of metal. Of course the metal-framed front has been, and is still, common enough ; but until now only as an outstanding protest against its own existence.

Plate xxxix is a simple and effective metal front. The plain flat brass bars seem quite suitable for their purpose and are at least much superior to those wooden elongated columns of some inch diameter whose abnormal proportions in the average shop are so markedly absurd.

The Crittal Manufacturing Co.'s front illustrated in Plate xl is unique in regard to the arrangements of the metal work which constitutes its frame, and which is a patent of the manufacturers. Its interests however, are not entirely confined to the metal framing, for the projecting bay over the front supported by some excellent consol brackets, is distinctly good ; while the plain surface provided for the lettering, enlarges the scale and interest of what is really a very small shop.

Most common of all materials, because most easily obtained and most easily adapted to the requirements of design, is the use of wood in connection with shop-fronts, teak, oak and mahogany especially being largely used. It will probably be some considerable time before the simple usefulness of these materials will be neglected as a means to a comparatively inexpensive and effective result. Naturally enough, it is easy to include a large number of excellent wooden and glass shop-fronts. These, while possessing no distinctive architectural value in regard to plan or form, are architecturally attractive, and their merit is made sufficiently prominent by the admirable character of their details alone. Among such fronts as these that designed by Mr. Paterson in Bond Street, London, and illustrated by Plate xli, is especially meritorious. This shop-front is of more than ordinary interest by reason of the fact that the architect has evidently found worthy inspiration for his design in an old shop-front at Lewes. Messrs. Sandorides are to be congratulated upon the possession of a front so thoroughly and artistically suitable.

The shop-front belonging to Messrs. Singers, at Paris (Plate xlii), has a peculiar interest of its own, insomuch as the detail is so characteristically French. Compare this front with Plate xliii, an English hairdresser's shop from London. Both fronts are carried out in wood, both are interesting and inspiring, yet it is hard to say which should be admired most; the straight and honest rigidity of treatment which marks the English front or the decorative freshness of the Louis detail in the Paris establishment.

Stewart and Co. (Plate xliv), and Spiking's (Plate xlv), are two typical examples of the very ordinary better class shop-front. Neither are markedly interesting or distinctive, but both have a quiet and sober effectiveness of their own which redeems them from the absolutely commonplace.

Glazing.

Plates xlvi and xlvii are both fronts with wooden frames, and indifferent detail, but both possessing those extraneous interests which are lent to a front by the introduction of a large quantity of curved glass. Ample inspiration has been found for these excesses of curvature, in the type of fronts owned by Messrs. Slater and Co., one of which is illustrated by Plate xxi.

Plate xlviii is a recessed front which has much merit, its chief interest, however, being contained by the uncommon arrangement of the glazing in the main window. This is bowed both horizontally and vertically and is believed to be quite unique in this respect.

Plates xxxix, xliv and xxvi show charming variations of leaded lights which add a graceful interest to what might otherwise be comparatively uninteresting designs. Indeed the height above seven or eight feet can generally be used for some such decorative accessory, as a leaded frieze. Another practical suggestion is shown by Plate xxxii. For here Luxfer lights have been introduced, adding immeasurably and at the same time not inartistically to the lighting of the shop interior.

The use of the wooden glazing bar plays an important part in making artistically interesting many of the fronts illustrated, notably Plates xlix, l, xxv and xxix. No better example of its effective use, however, can be found than the charming design by Mr. George Walton, for The Kodak Co., in Brussels (Plate li). Especially noticeable is the clever way in which the architect has, by means of the glazing bar, given a charming bowed effect to the main window while at the same time using only flat glass. Quite excellent, too, is the introduction of some simple lead glazing in the main frieze above the transome. This design is really superlatively good.

Lettering.

In regard to lettering, the neglect accorded to the sign-painter's art is to be deplored. The lettering of most fronts in the streets of to-day is either intolerably ugly or artistically unintelligible. Surely a creditable and intelligent interest can be given to a shop-front by well-proportioned figure work of good design. Painted letters in deeply shadowed perspective should certainly be avoided, because, however cleverly they may be done, they are not quite honest enough to be strictly architectural. Precisely the same effect can be obtained by planting raised letters of a suitable colour and material directly on to the painted fascia board (Plates xl, li, xxvi, l, and xvi).

There are a large number of specially made letters available for use in connection with shop fascia boards. These are made in wood, celluloid, white enamelled, copper, prismatic cut glass, and various other materials. Very popular with a certain class of shop-front is the use of the well-known Brilliant Letter. This is concave (V-shaped) in section, and made of stout sheet copper stamped from steel dies, and as a rule gilded. It is doubtful though if anything can be more simple and effective than the plain painted letter—preferably white on a green ground—as shown in Plate xxxi. In regard to the fascia board, the tilting of this towards the street is surely an artistic mistake ; for it has a tendency to throw the building illusively out of perspective, and to distort the lines of proportion. Perhaps it would not be too much to suggest doing away with it in its present position, for more often than not its use as a name-board is valueless. Often it is too high to be read, or else it is partly or wholly hidden by the sun-blind. The name of the shopkeeper might be more effectively disposed along the transome, which has already been indicated should limit the height of the display area. If this space be occupied by the sun-blind, the name might be placed in a prominent position over the door. An illustration of this is to be found in Plate xvi, while the name cleverly used along the limiting transome is illustrated in Plate xxvii.

In such a brief essay as this, no abstract æsthetic complaint need be entered against the prevalent tendency to conceal the supporting girder by a wooden fascia. Note might be taken of the method the late Mr. Waterhouse adopted in a shop in Glasgow. The girder was left entirely exposed, and the name of the shopkeeper, in bold metal letters, was bolted to the girder, and the whole carefully coppered. The result was a complete success, and the idea is worthy of more frequent use. Where it is absolutely necessary for the name to be in the usual position, it is not essential that the fascia should be in wood. Many mosaic fascias are now carried out as in Plates xlvii, xxviii, xxxviii, and xxi. These are generally made complete in one slab on a thick cement backing, reinforced with expanded metal. Fascias in incised glass, marble, metal, and a large number of other materials are made in wood frames all complete. These are easy for fixing to a plain wood fascia. Such fascias as these are shown in Plates xliii and xlvi. Stall-board plates of a similar nature are also largely used. A modelled plaster fascia gives great scope for some excellent work, a particularly good example being illustrated by Plate xxxvi.

It is the custom to place the name of the shop-owner on the sill or stall-plate, which is sometimes above the stall-board, but which, more often than not, takes the place of the stall-board. Figure 19 shows a more effective alternative to this. A wooden frame containing the name of the shopkeeper is placed behind the window and sloping away from it. Goods are thus not likely to be placed too close to the window, and if necessary the sign can be made transparent and a light placed behind it at night.

Lighting.

A consideration of the lighting of the shop-front is important enough to call for a few remarks in connection therewith. The general principles should be towards the realization of a softly-toned light, sufficient in regard to quantity, but being evenly distributed rather than concentrated in garish and powerful arc or other big lamps. What light is required outside the shop should be so treated as to be in keeping with the governing characteristics of the design, yet it need not be a large amount of light. All that seems really necessary is that the name of the shop-keeper shall at least be sufficiently apparent. This might be accomplished either by the use of illuminated hanging signs as shown in Plates xx and xxxi, or by an arrangement of reflecting electric lamps fixed at the base of the fascia board (Plate xxxv). Better than the latter however, would be the use of some sort of transparent fascia board which at night could be illuminated from behind. It is well to know that the London County Council require in regard to external lamps for shop windows "that the underside portion must not be less than 8ft. from the pavement, the extreme projection over the public way not exceeding 3ft. when the width of the pavement permits, and not less than 2ft. from the carriage-way. The external dimensions of such lamps must not exceed 2ft. 3in. in any direction." In regard to the lighting of the interior of the window itself, a collaboration with a good electrical engineer is undoubtedly the best method to be adopted in regard to the disposition of the various points. For it must be remembered that the needs of the various trades largely govern the amount and disposition of the light in a shop window.

Plate lii has a unique arrangement in regard to the lighting of the shop window. Quaint lamps of wonderful design are hung over the window case and in the recess formed above the main transome. This throws a protected and admirably shaded light directly on to the goods. The result is as successful as it deserves to be and the idea is worthy of frequent imitation. A working drawing of this design is shown by Figure 18.

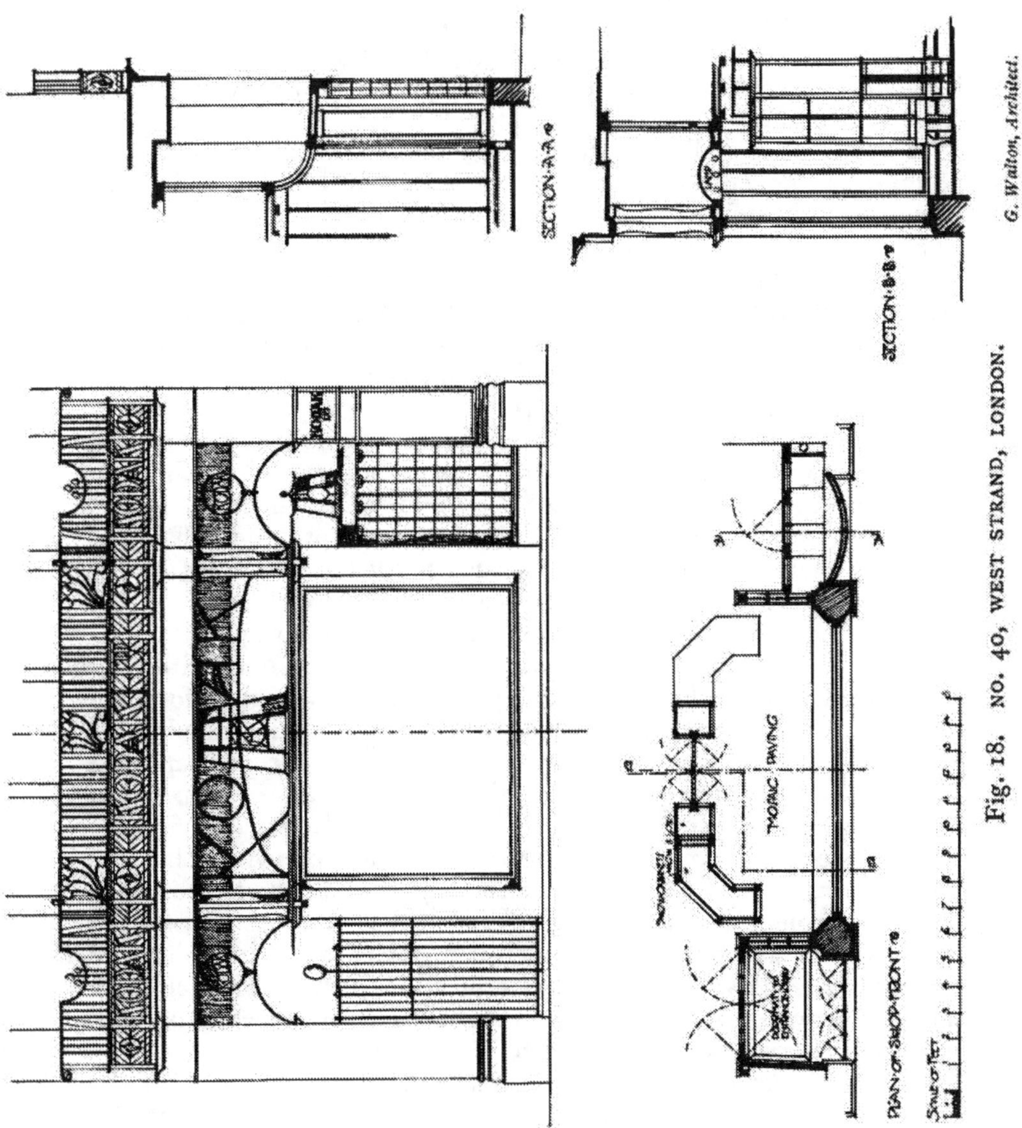

G. Walton, Architect.

Fig. 18. NO. 40, WEST STRAND, LONDON.

Construction.

Figure 19 shows a plan, elevation and section of a typical shop-front. It must be added that this shop-front is included not for any particular architectural merit it may possess, but simply because it is helpful in making quite clear the ordinary difficulties of construction common to all kinds of shop-fronts.

It would be as well to remember the restrictions placed upon the designer by the various local authorities, both in London and in the provinces. Thus in regard to the projection of cornices, etc., the London Building Act requires: "In a street or way of a width not greater than thirty feet, any shop-front may project beyond the external wall of the building to which it belongs to any extent not exceeding five inches, and any cornice of any such shop-front may project to any extent not exceeding thirteen inches; and in any street or way of a width greater than thirty feet, any shop-front may project to any extent not exceeding ten inches, and any cornice of any such shop-front may project to any extent not exceeding eighteen inches beyond the external wall of the building to which it belongs, over the ground of the owner of the building, provided that this provision shall not authorise in any such street the projection of any part of any such shop-front other than the cornice on or over the public way or any land to be given up to the public way."

It will be noted that this portion of the act deals only with projections in so far as they encroach upon or over the public footpath or that portion of the owners' land which might be intended to be given over to the public foot-path. In regard to the projection of shop-fronts upon the owners' land alone special clauses with regard to the making of such fronts free from the dangers of fire are very properly enforced and covered by the following clauses: "Where any part of a building which is used or adapted to be used as a shop projects for a distance of seven feet or more beyond the main front of any building of which it forms part and in which any persons are employed or sleep the projecting portion of such shop shall be provided by the owner with a roof constructed of fire-resisting materials not less than five inches thick.

"It shall be lawful to construct or place in or upon the roof of the portion of any shop so projecting beyond the main front of the building as aforesaid lantern-lights or ventilating-cowls. Provided that no such lantern-light or ventilating-cowl shall be constructed

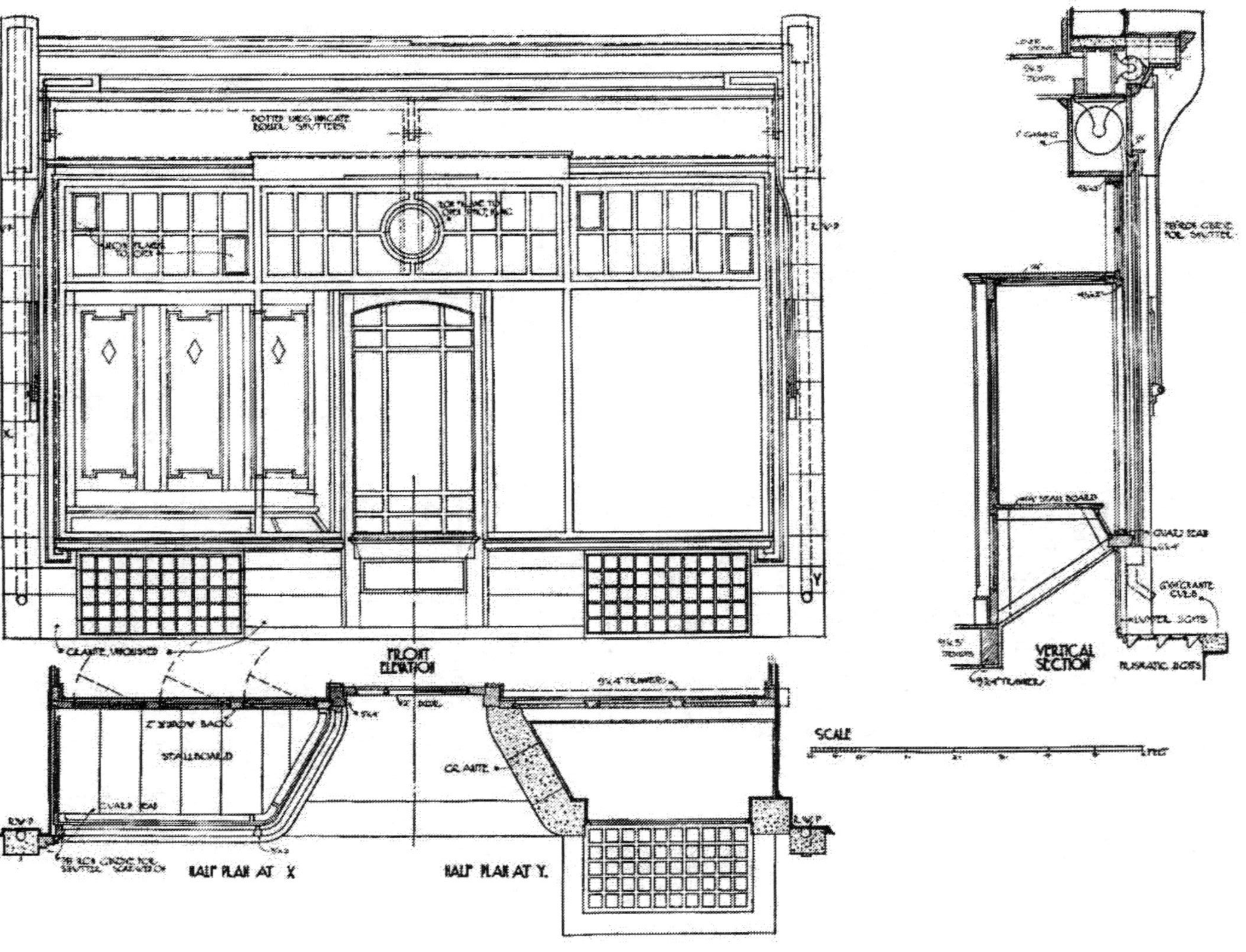

Fig. 19. PLAN, ELEVATION AND SECTION OF A TYPICAL SHOP-FRONT.

or placed so that any part thereof will be at a less distance than six feet from the main front of the building from which the shop projects or within such distance as may be reasonable in the circumstances of the case from any other external or party wall. Provided also that the sides of such lantern-light or ventilating-cowl (except the side facing away from the main building) shall be carried up in fire-resisting materials for two feet above the roof in or upon which it is constructed or placed. Provided further that no part of any such lantern-light or ventilating-cowl shall project above the roof in or upon which the same is constructed or placed to a greater extent than five feet."

There are some further enactments with reference to projecting fronts, requiring that suitable access shall be gained to the roofs of same and also ensuring that proper guards or parapets shall be provided in the case of flat-roofed projections.

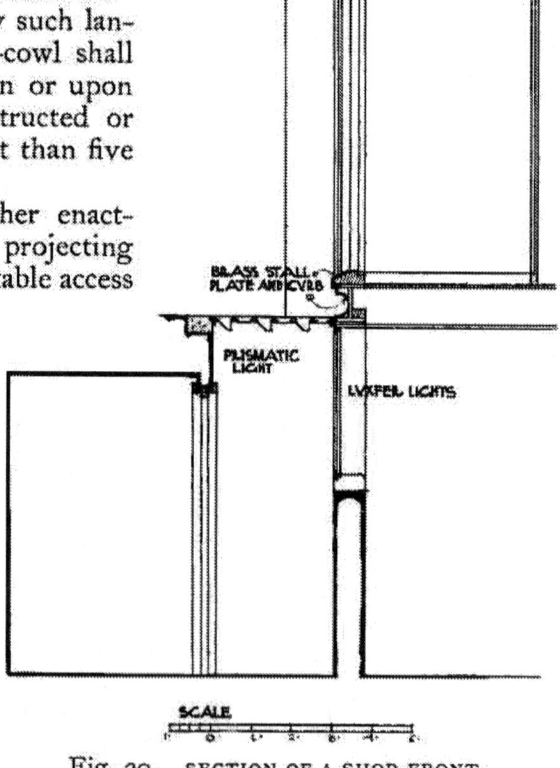

Fig. 20. SECTION OF A SHOP-FRONT.

Returning to a consideration of the typical front, it must not be forgotten in designing it that the woodwork shall not be fixed nearer than four inches to the centre of the party-wall where the adjoining premises are separated by a party wall, or nearer than four inches to the face of the wall of the adjoining premises, where the adjoining premises have a separate wall, unless a fire proof pier four inches wide at the least is placed in between and as high as the whole front.

It will be noticed in Figure 19, that rolled steel-joists support the main walls of the building and are covered in with a regulation fascia-board fixed to rough bracketing. There is a tendency when the fascia-board is of considerable width and length for it to cast, and attention should be given to this point. Iron tubes inserted through and across the board at intervals of three feet will prevent this ; or the board can be grooved and keyed with hard-wood strips. As an alternative to the rolled-steel joists Figure 20 shows a front supported by a reinforced concrete lintel with a stone cornice above. The lettering is fastened directly on to the front of this lintel, and much superfluous woodwork is thus done away with. The sun-blind, it will be noticed, is contained in a boxed transome cutting across the front at a height of seven or eight feet.

The lead-covered flat to the fascia-board when very wide, should fall towards the building and a proper secret gutter provided at the back with the necessary falls. It is undesirable in any case that the water should be allowed to drip over the front on to the pavement below. In fact the London Building Act, 1894, section 73, clause 7, especially provides against this contingency. The water is usually taken along to a cesspool at the end and a lead pipe from there conducts it to a rain-water pipe, taken down as a rule behind the side pilaster. Figure 19 shows the plate-glass of the main windows glazed directly into the shop frame. Sometimes, however, sashes are provided as well as the main framing, but more often than not the section of the corner is a very light hard-wood slip with shifting fillets.

Stall-Boards and Pavement Lights.

The combination of stall-board and pavement lights must necessarily be considered together, although the exigencies of design which modern commercial requirements demand have almost precluded the use of any stall-board. Figures 20, 21, 23 and 25 indicate several varieties of stall-board and pavement lights which may be adopted according to the circumstances of each case.

Figure 20 is an arrangement where a stall-board light is impossible. It shows ordinary pavement lights in connection with a partition in the basement glazed in its upper portion with Luxfer Lucidux or similar lights. The light from the pavement prisms strikes the Lucidux and is refracted into the main cellar. The partition forms a convenient division between the basement proper and such w.c.'s, lavatories, etc., that might possibly be placed in the vault formed under the pavement. Where there is no excavation under the pavement, an arrangement like Figure 21 might conveniently be adopted. The stall-board light is filled with clear glass. It is desirable that the beam or girder supporting the floor, and the beam supporting the inner edge of the pavement should be shallow, in order to obstruct the light as little as possible. Figure 25 shows a case where a pavement light is not admissible, but where there is an opportunity of utilizing the space afforded by a high stall-board. The stall-board light is glazed with clear glass and a sub-canopy of Luxfer lights fitted below. The sub-canopy should be hinged so as to allow of the upper sides of same being cleaned.

Figure 23 shows a stall-board light, pavement light, and a sub-canopy used in connection with a recessed shop-front. Here the sub-canopy is also hinged, and this allows for the use of cellar flaps instead of a fixed pavement light. It should be pointed out that an easy opportunity is afforded by the stall-board light of providing for some ventilation to the basement.

With regard to the position of the

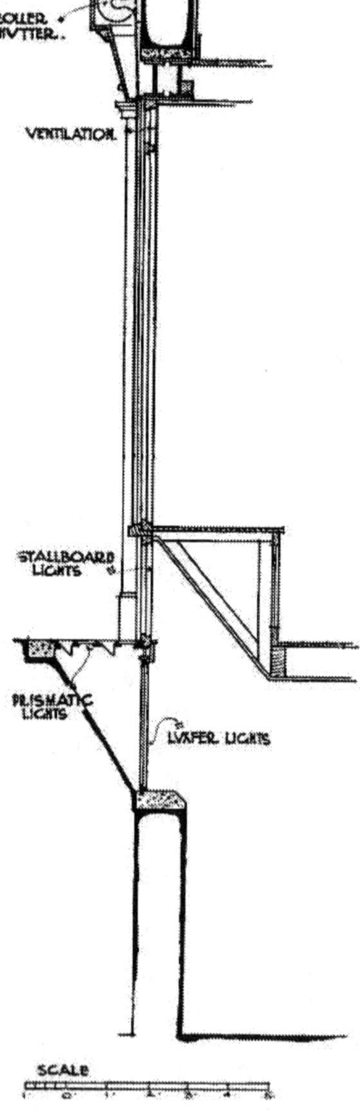

Fig. 21. SECTION OF A SHOP-FRONT.

pavement light, insomuch as certain bye-laws and certain authorities in different towns object to the projection of the basement under the pavement, there are almost insuperable difficulties in the way of providing the necessary amount of light.

Under such circumstances a recessed shop-front would provide ample and abundant space for pavement lights, it being quite possible to deal with these in an artistic and suitable fashion, by so planning them as to form part of an architectural and geometrical

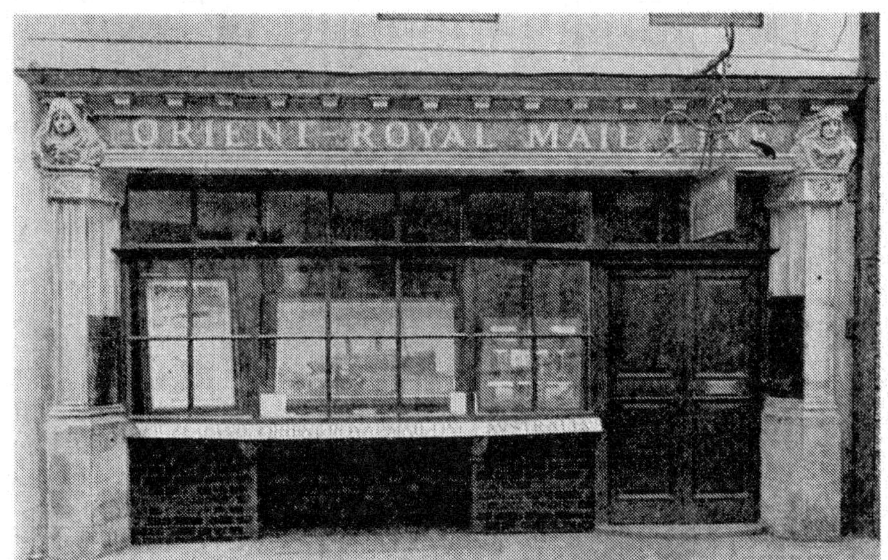

Fig. 22. NO. 18 COCKSPUR STREET, LONDON.

pattern of tiles and lights to fill up completely the loggia or recess. Plates xvi and xx better illustrate this point.

In the clever and original little shop-front belonging to the Orient Pacific Mail Line (Figure 22), we notice another treatment of the pavement light which is at once interesting and suggestive. Here there was no opportunity, as in the case of the recessed shop-front, of utilizing the loggia for pavement lights. A small recess under the actual shop-frame was formed in glazed brick, and the floor of this small recess fitted with a pavement light. Thus the lights by being placed back in such a way are not walked upon and broken by the traffic of the pavements.

In regard to the height of the stall-board, this, naturally enough, is regulated by the nature of the design and the needs of the trade. There seems little use, however, for the usual custom of taking the glass practically down to the ground. A little thought must naturally show, that, beyond tailors, drapers and kindred businesses, there is no need to sacrifice the undoubted usefulness of the stall-board light for the sake of having the glass so low. Even in the case of a modern draper whose shop floor is usually about a foot above the ground, it would be advisable, if possible, to create some hollow instead of the usual stone or metal curb which divides the glass from the pavement (Figure 20). Thus a customer can peer through the glass quite close up to the front and at the same time there is not any inconvenient kicking of the feet against an awkwardly designed curb. It is notable that in many of the fronts illustrated the space under the stall-board is built in with glazed tiles or faience. This is good, for the introduction of subdued colouring must at all times be artistically advantageous.

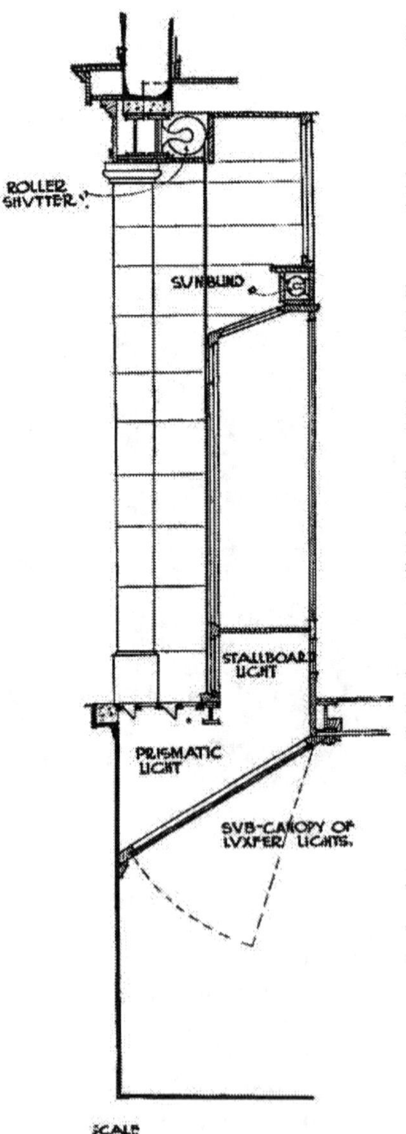

Fig. 23. SECTION OF A RECESSED SHOP-FRONT.

Sun Blinds and Roller Shutters.

With the recessed front, provided the recess is deep enough, very little is needed in the way of a sun-blind, but where, as in the case of the shop-front belonging to Messrs. Martin Bros. (Plate xvii), the recess is small and the height considerable, a mid-day sun easily strikes upon the lower portion of the shop window. This has unconsciously been partly provided for. A wide shelf limits the height of effective display and projecting out sufficiently helps to lessen the angle at which the rays of the sun strike the lower portion of the shop window. Of course the projection of this shelf might not be great enough to completely shade the goods in the window. In that case a small sun-blind of short width could conveniently be fixed within the box-like transome or shelf which would strike across the elevation of the window at a height of about seven to eight feet. Such an arrangement is illustrated by Figure 23. It is worth recording that Mr. George R. Sims, in a characteristic protest against the dull dreariness and lack of colour in important streets and shops, sees no reason why more attention should not be given to the sun-blind as a means of enlivening the drab monotony of tone. He suggests that the sun-blind might be striped in various bright but harmonious colours.

Figures 19, 20, 21, 23, and 25 show various positions in which the sun-blinds and roller-shutters of a front can conveniently be fixed. In regard to the latter, perhaps some little explanation is required. Sometimes they are made in iron, but more often they are manufactured from the best pine, in uniform convex laths, morticed and connected with steel or copper bands. Also they are connected by means of strong straining webs. The shutters are fixed to stout barrel cases containing steel spiral springs of a strong nature, these springs acting throughout the entire breadth of the shutter, and bearing on the central spindle of the shutter. If necessary the shutters can be worked by balance weights or other similar motions, but as a rule the strength of the spring, which is strained when the shutter is opened, is strong enough to make the closing of the shutter an easy matter, the tendency being for the spring to resume its normal position. It is desirable to provide the following space for the shutters to coil in :

For shutter	6 to 8 feet high	. .	10 inches.
„ „	10 to 11 „	. .	12 „
„ „	11 to 12 „	. .	13 „
„ „	13 to 14 „	. .	14 „

The sash styles or pilasters at either side should allow for the insertion of a $\frac{7}{8}$in. iron groove for the shutter to work in. This groove must be securely screwed to the styles as shown in Figure 19. Specially made iron brackets are attached to the girders as shown in Figures 19, 23, and 25, or built into the wall above as in Figure 21. Usually these are about seven feet apart, but this distance, of course, can be varied to the needs of special positions. The dotted lines indicated in Figure 19 represent movable metal strips placed in position below the supporting brackets of the shutters, and having grooved edges in which the free ends of the shutters run. It is necessary to remove these pieces when the shutters are not protecting the shop.

Steel revolving shutters are recommended for banks, jewellers, and similar classes of tradesmen ; also shops where additional protection in case of fire is needed. Attention must be given to the provision of suitable guard beads, as shown in Figure 19, to prevent the chance of possible friction between the glass and the roller shutter. The boxing for the sun-blind should allow sufficient room for the roller or barrel. This is made in stout tin, properly jointed, and filled with a hardwood cylinder throughout its length. It bears upon a stout iron spindle, and the movement of the roller is by conical steel springs, which should be at least 5ft. long. The diameter of the roller varies according to the frontage, thus :

9 to 12 feet	. .	3 inches.
12 to 15 „	. .	3½ „
15 to 18 „	. .	4 „
18 to 22 „	. .	4½ „

The blind material is similar to sail-cloth, and made of flax, properly attached to the roller, and fixed to the front lath with a stout tongue or fillet secured by zinc nails. If the blind has to project more than 7ft., it is necessary to mount the supporting irons on sliding plates. Generally, however, projecting arms with forged straps to attach to the lath, and forged eyes working on bolt pins in malleable cast iron shoe plates fixed to the side pilasters are all that are required.

ENTRANCES.

Not the least important part of the shop-front is the door and its fitments. In a shop where there is a constant stream of customers it is extremely desirable that some attention should be given to the problem of protecting against the dangerous swinging of hollow hung or other such doors. In large drapers' and kindred establishments a commissionaire or boy is often kept to open and close the doors after a customer. This seems an ineffective and expensive method. Again, swing doors of the ordinary type are draughty and no protection from the entry of dust and noise from the street. There is always inconvenience with them, and their "push" and "pull" notices are generally sufficiently perplexing to ensure the collision of two people, one going out, and one going in. Figure 24 is a

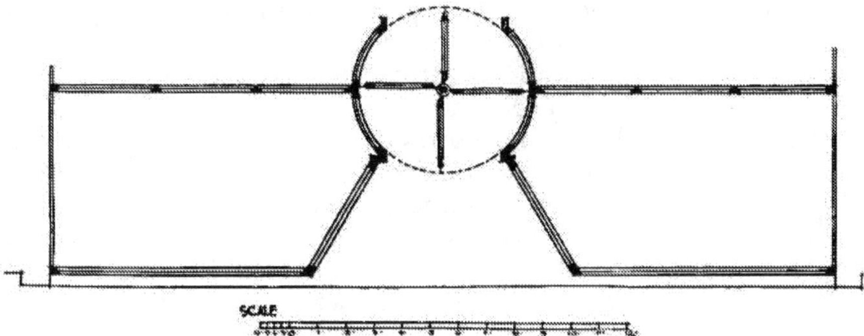

Fig. 24. PLAN OF A SHOP-FRONT WITH REVOLVING DOORS.

plan of a shop-front where the now familiar revolving door of the Van Kennel Co. is in use. The advantages of these doors are now well recognised and their adoption for large shop-fronts is advisable where expense is not a primary consideration. Of course in a small front the door need be no more than an ordinary glass-door hung to rebated frames. In larger fronts, however, it is sometimes found convenient to form a vestibule in the shop and thus have two pairs of doors. Such a lobby should, of course, be sufficiently roomy. Two doors, one in and one out, are sometimes placed with a pier between.

Condensation.

Much thought has been given to the difficulty which is always cropping up of how to prevent the condensation of the moisture upon the inside of the shop window, and it seems that a completely satisfactory solution is as far off as ever. Theoretically the problem is quite easy of solution: for it is only necessary to keep the temperature inside the window the same as that outside. To do this, however, the external air must be allowed to circulate freely inside the shop window and the difficulty of admitting it without also admitting a good deal of dust is a very pregnant one, and by no means solved by the crude expediency of a small ventilating grating at the top of the shop-front. The use of certain preparations containing glycerine as their basis have been used upon the inside of the glass. They are however, only partially successful. Another and more expensive method is the use of Bunsen burners fixed at the base of the window. These send a constant current of dry warm air up and near the surface of the glass, and prevent, unless the air inside the window is very humid, the objectional condensation and steaming of the windows. It is desirable that the air in the actual window shall be completely disconnected from that in the shop by glass screens at the back and top. A current of air from the outside might then be introduced below the window-sill as shown in Figure 25, while an extractor fixed at the top as shown would tend to the full circulation of a current of air of the same temperature as that outside. Very little difficulty would then be experienced in regard to windows steaming. It has been found that hot-water pipes below the stall-board have kept the air in the window-case sufficiently dry to prevent very largely the evils of condensation.

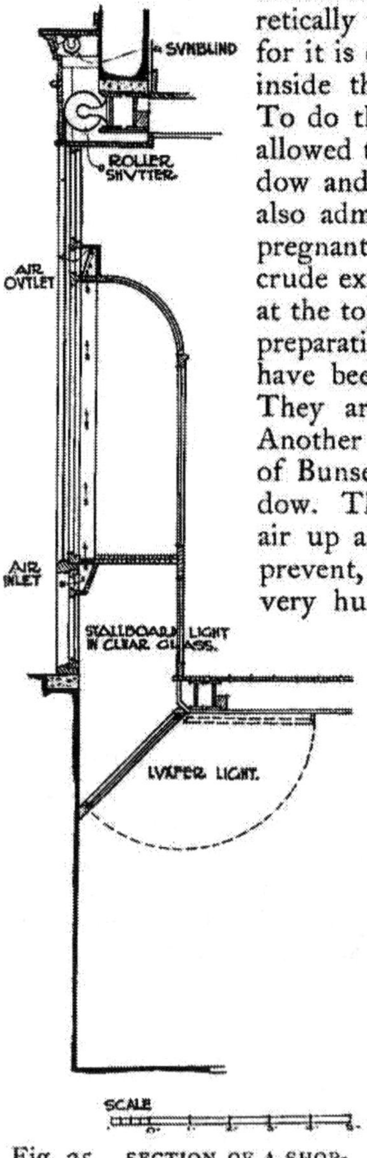

Fig. 25. SECTION OF A SHOP-FRONT.

Plate 36.

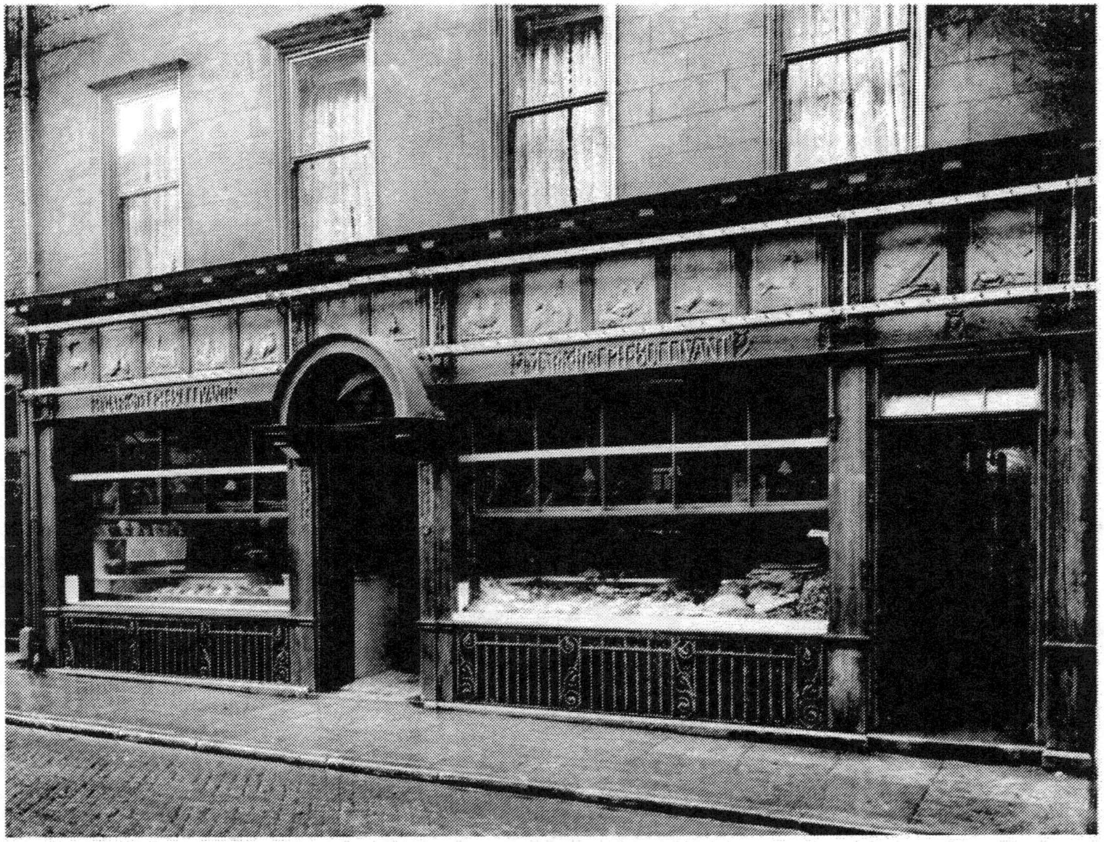

FEASEGATE, YORK.

Plate 37.

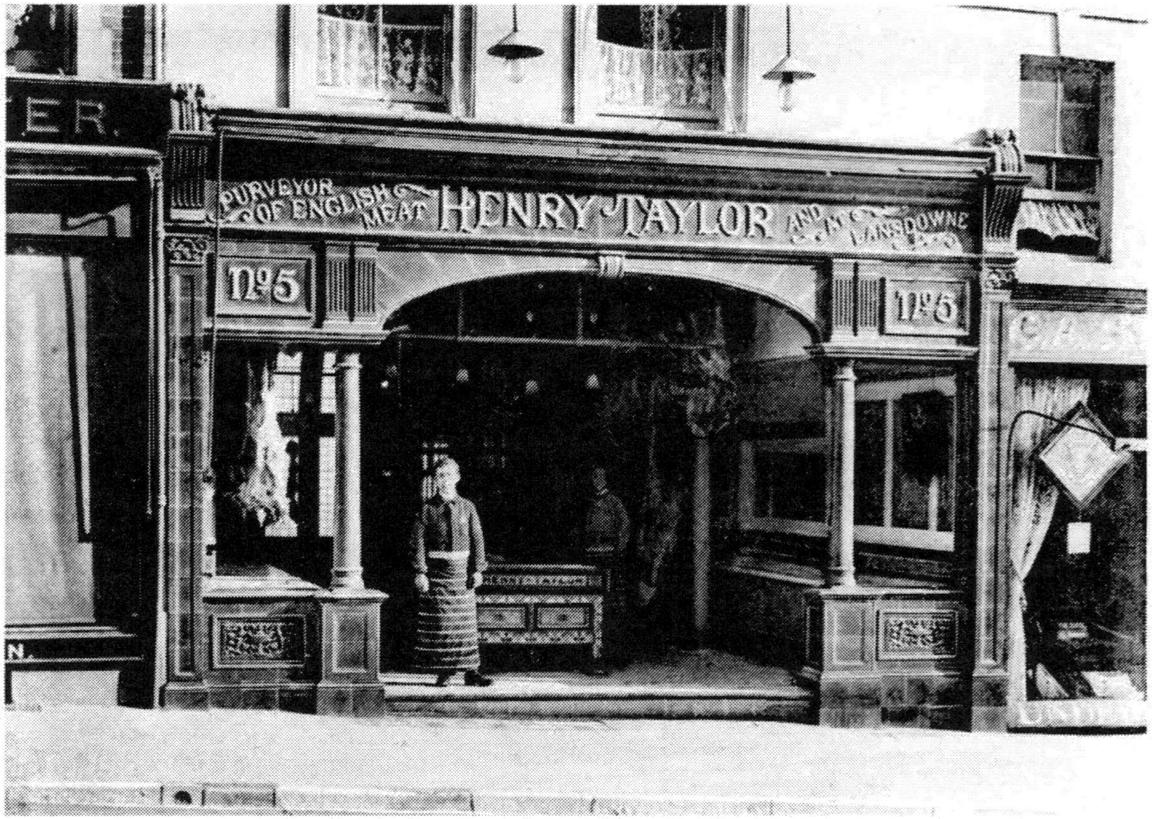

NO. 5, COMMERCIAL STREET, BOURNEMOUTH.

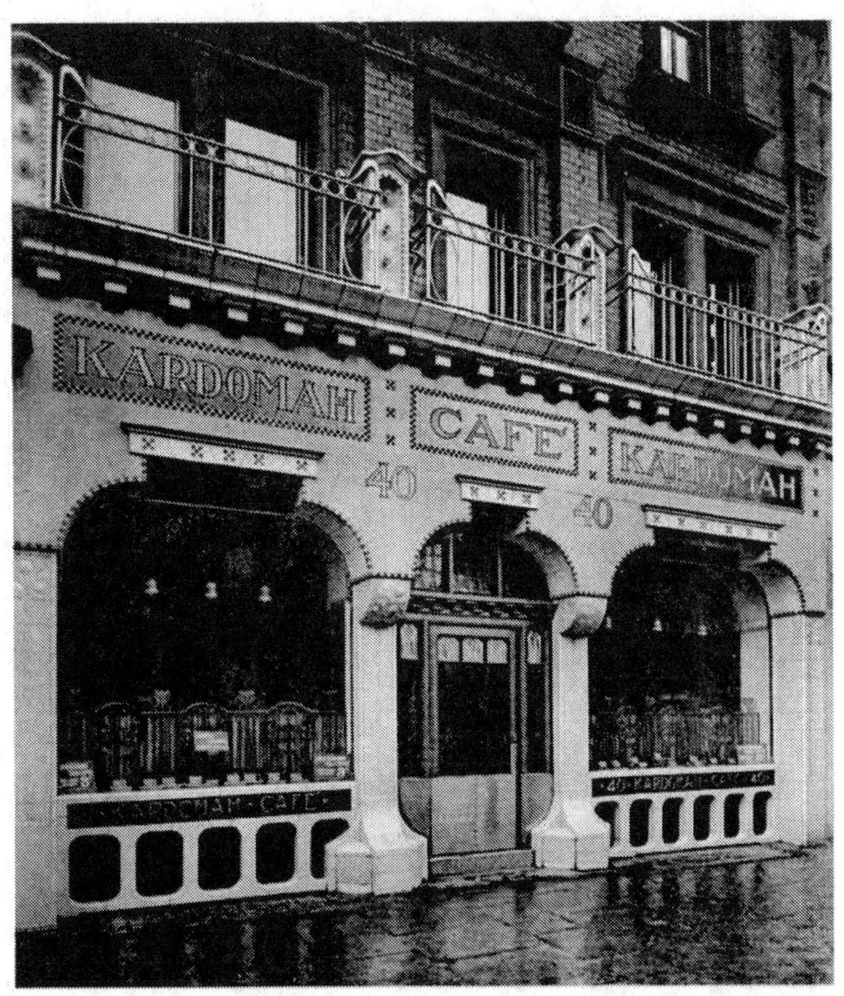

NO. 42, DALE STREET, LIVERPOOL.

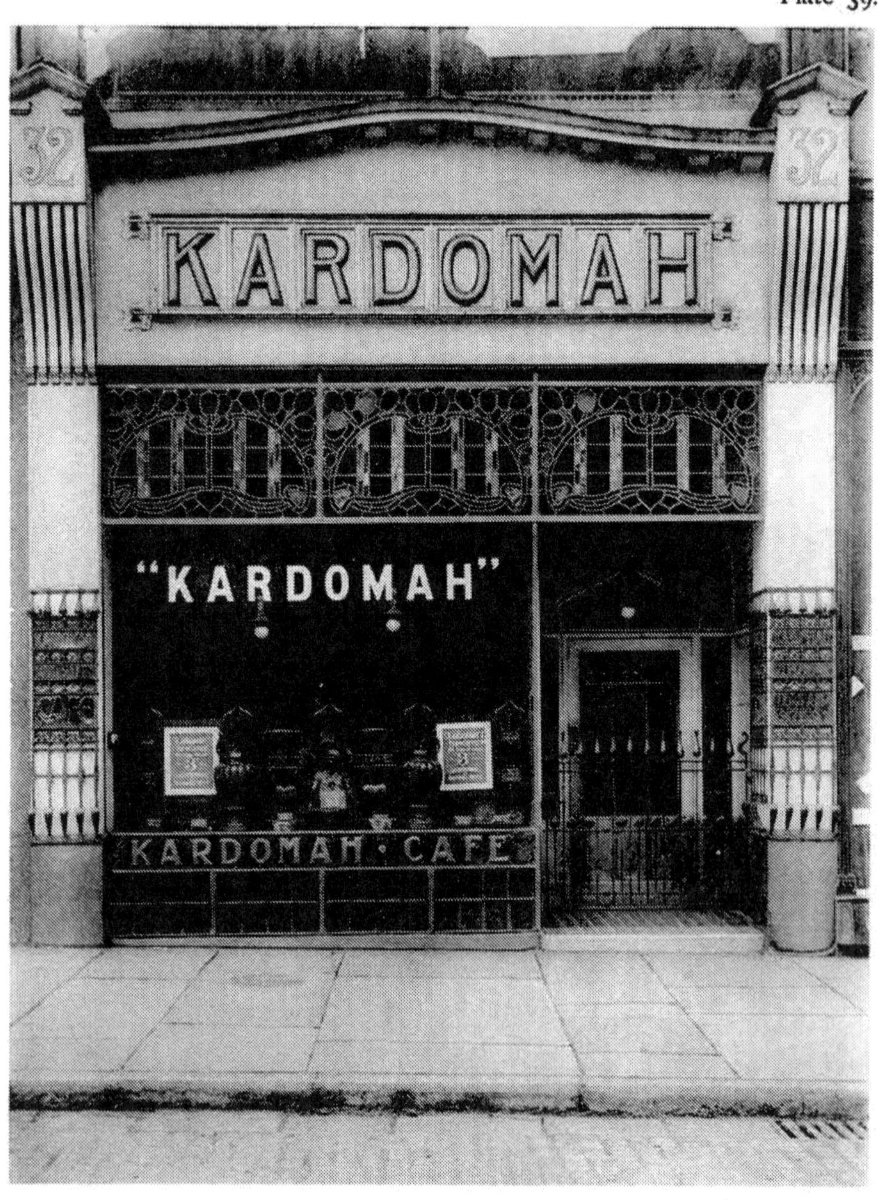

CHURCH STREET, LIVERPOOL

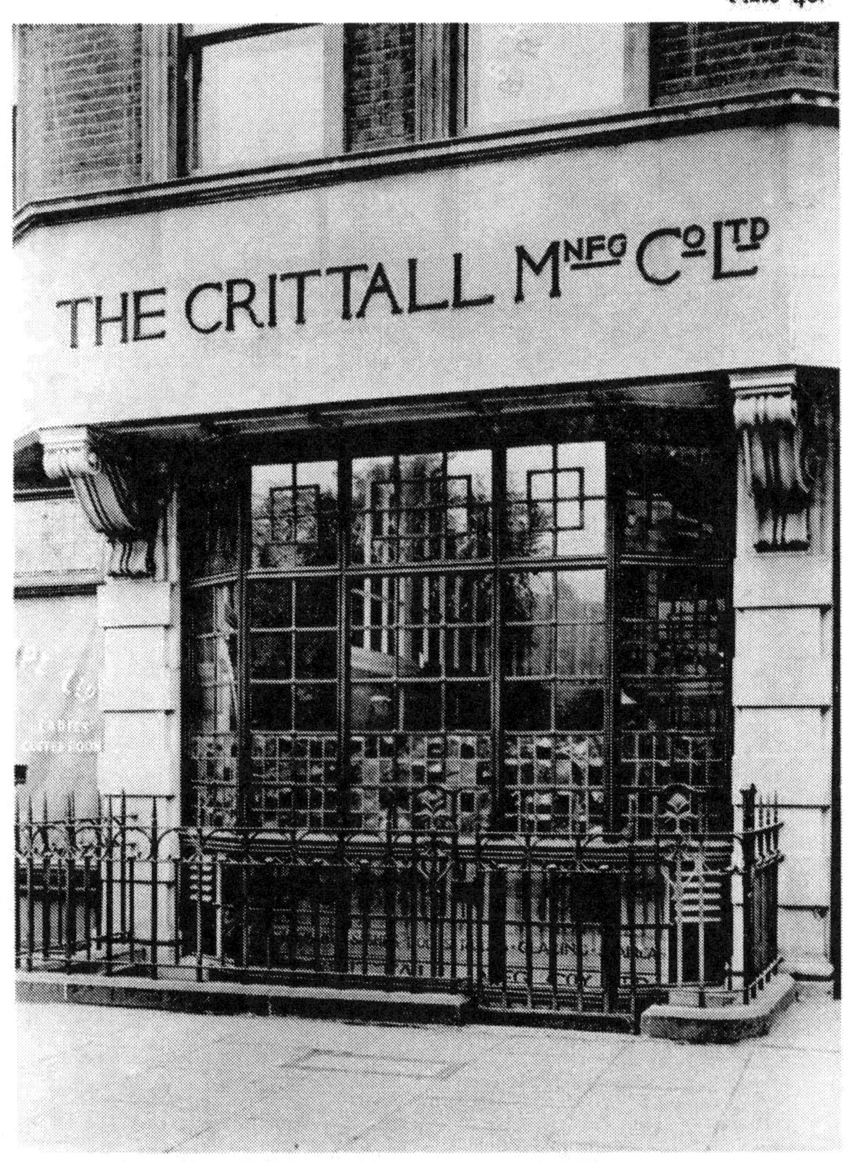

NOS. 11 & 12, FINSBURY SQUARE, LONDON.

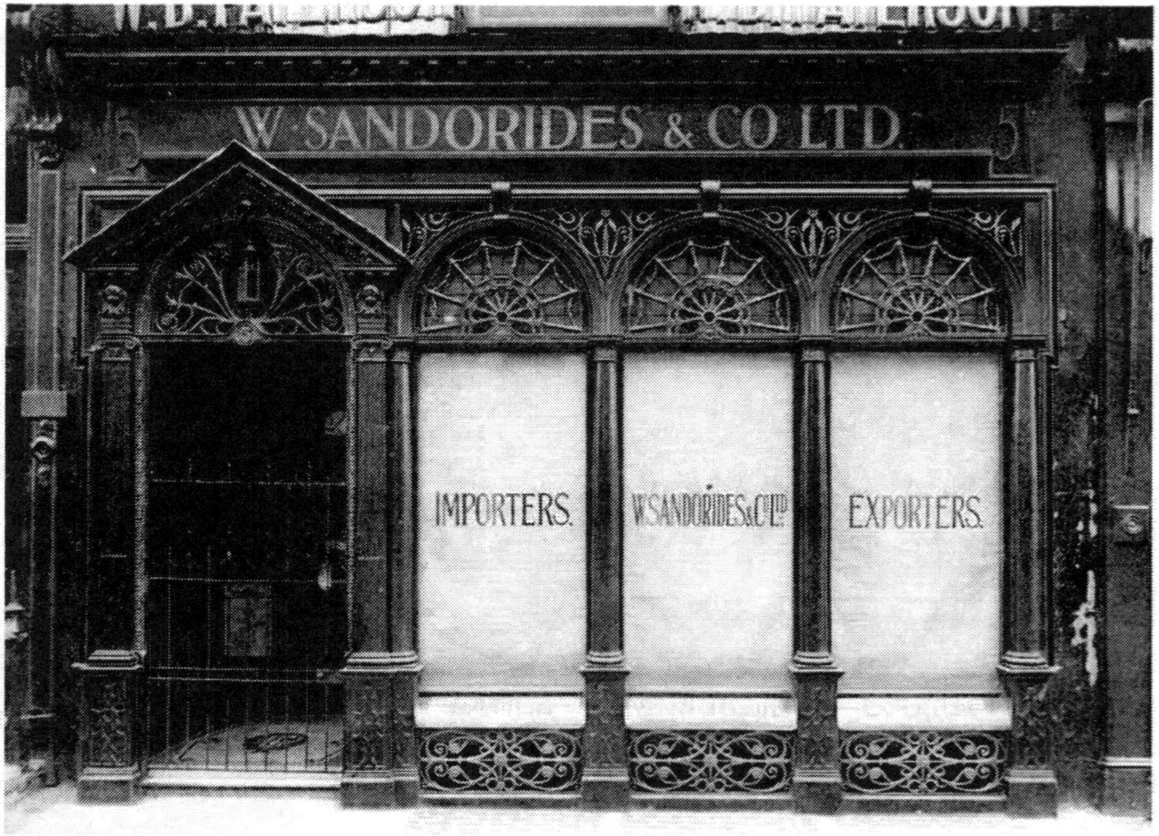

Plate 41.

NO. 5, OLD BOND STREET, LONDON.

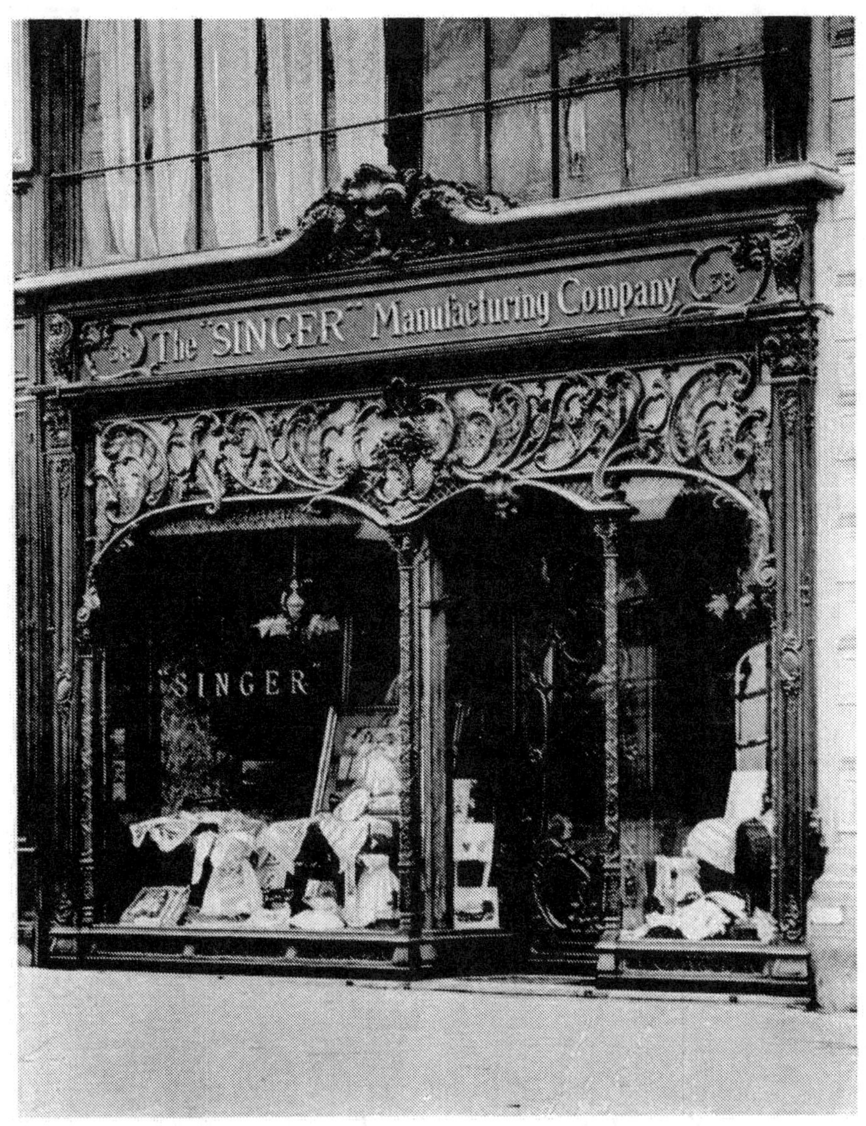

THE SINGER MANUFACTURING CO., PARIS.

Plate 43.

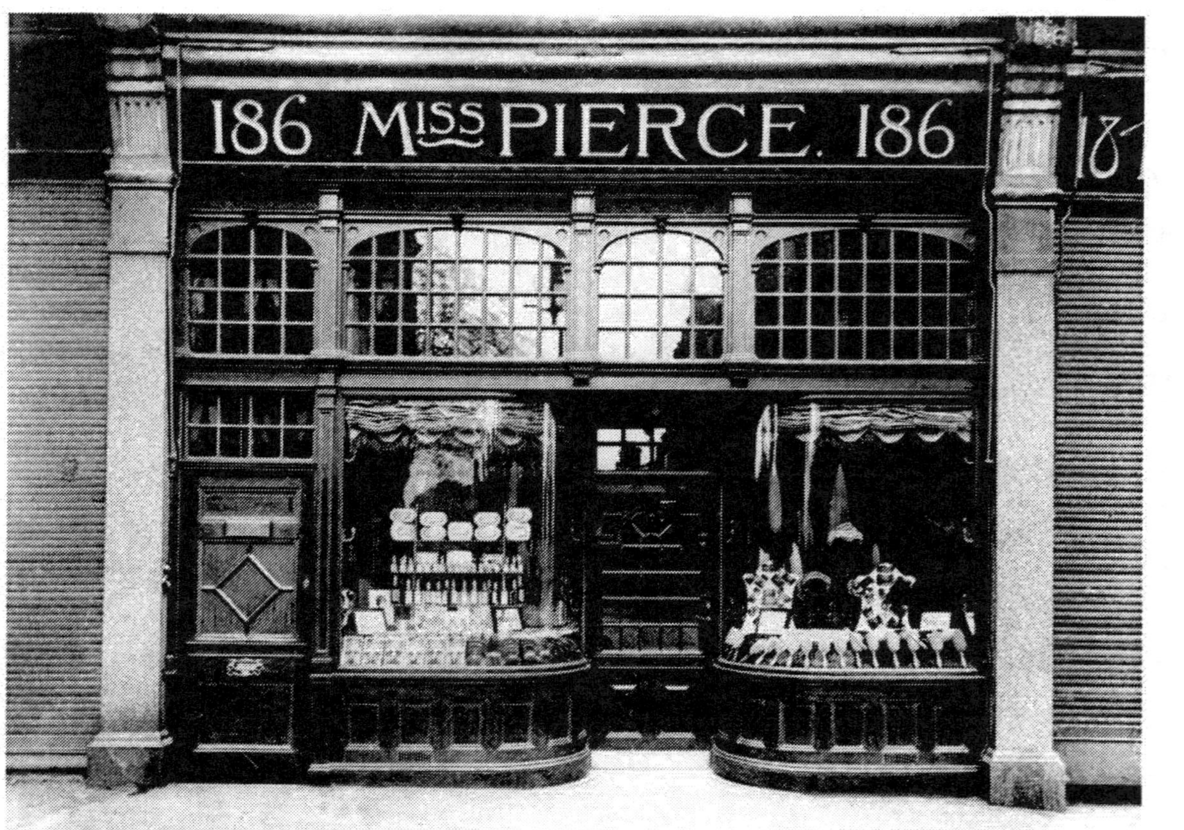

NO. 186, FINCHLEY ROAD, LONDON.

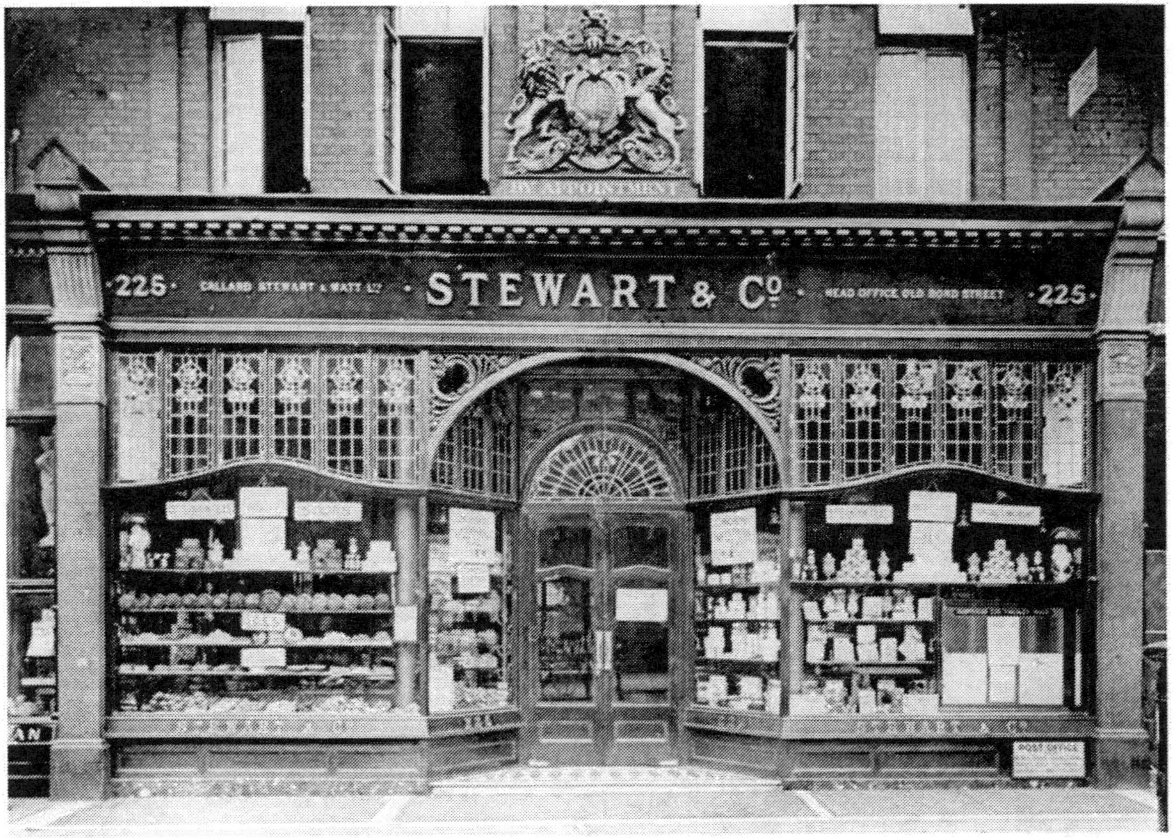

Plate 44.

NO. 225, FINCHLEY ROAD, LONDON.

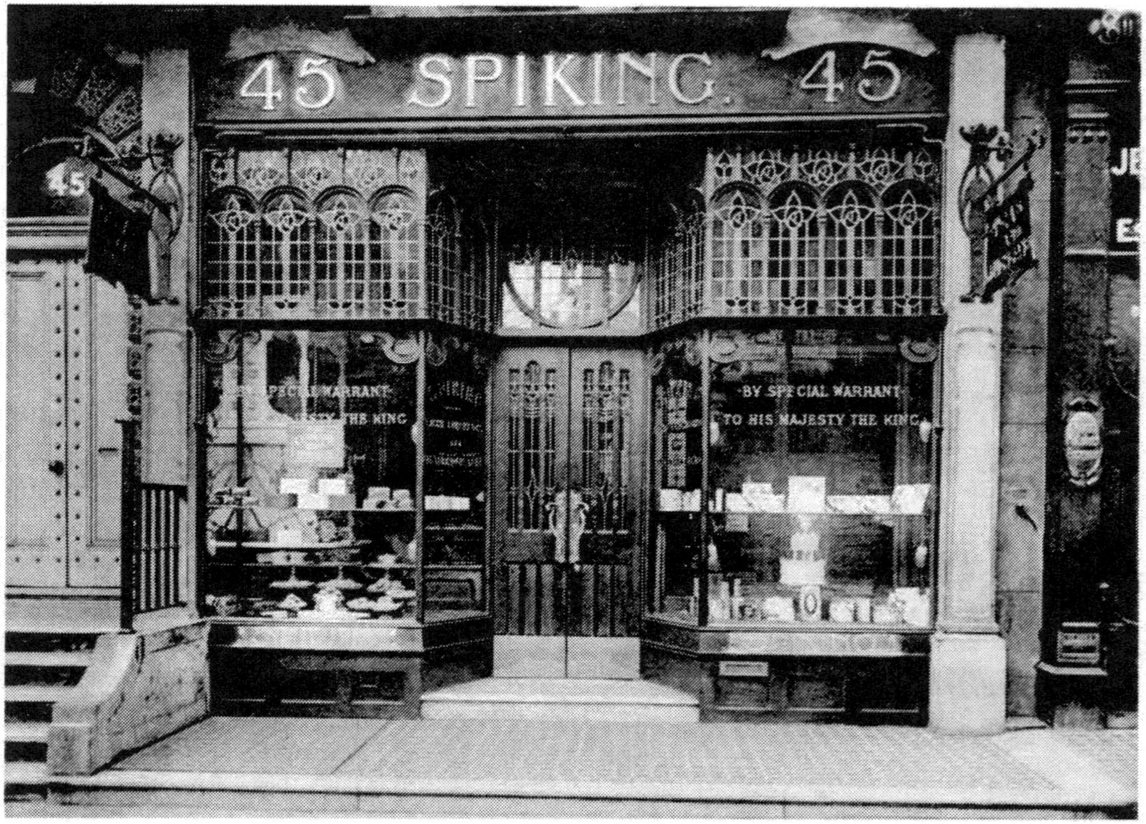

NO. 45, DOVER STREET, LONDON.

Plate 46.

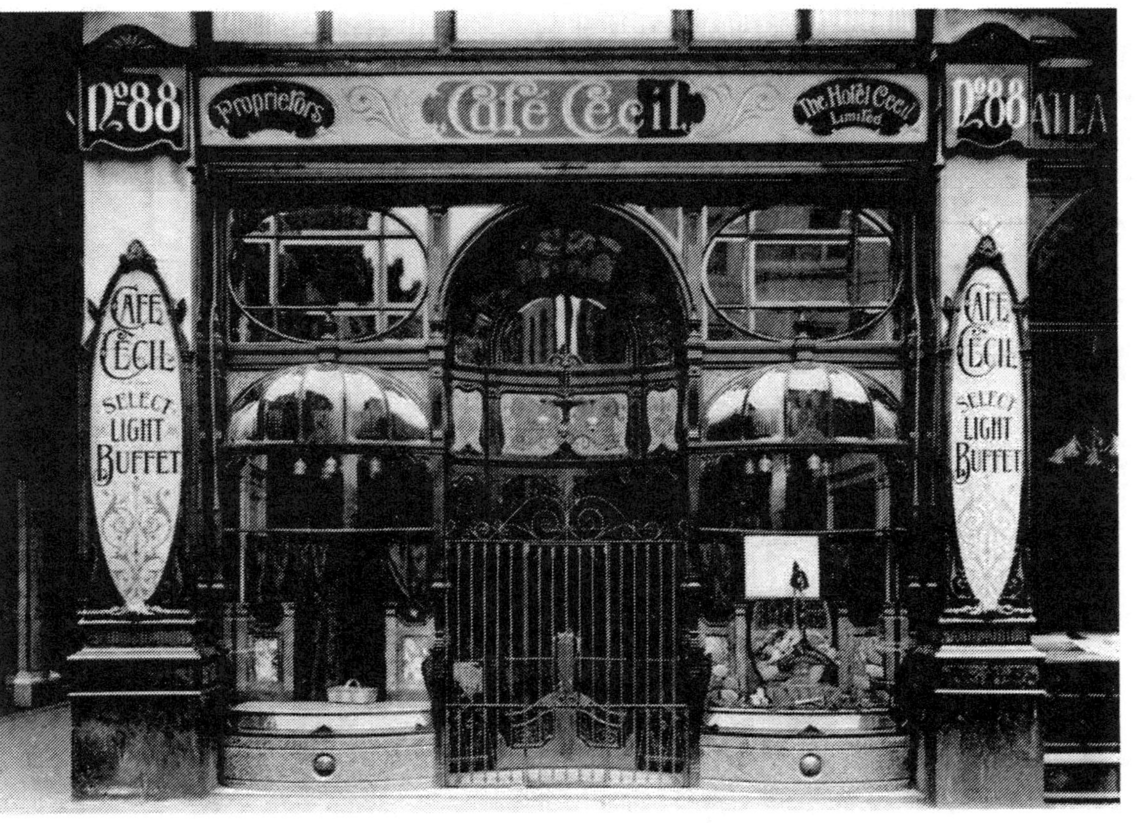

NO. 88, STRAND, LONDON.

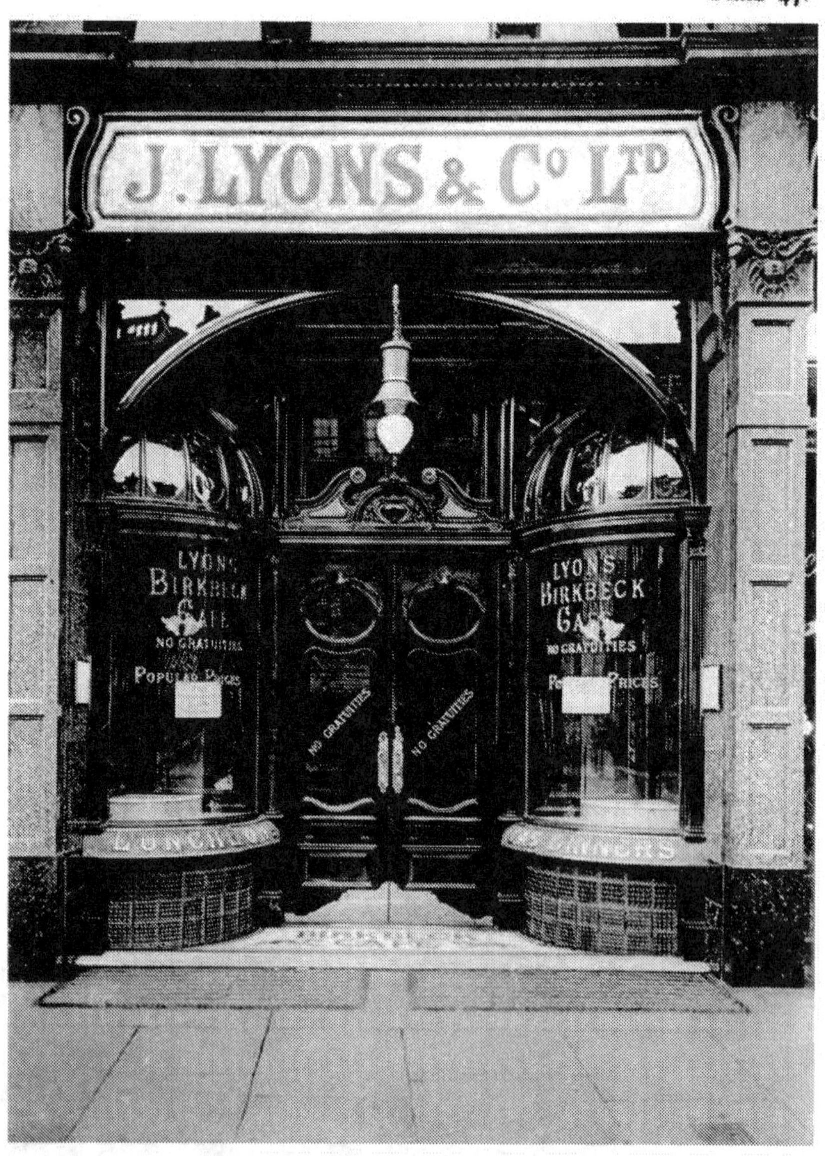

NO. 329, HIGH HOLBORN, LONDON.

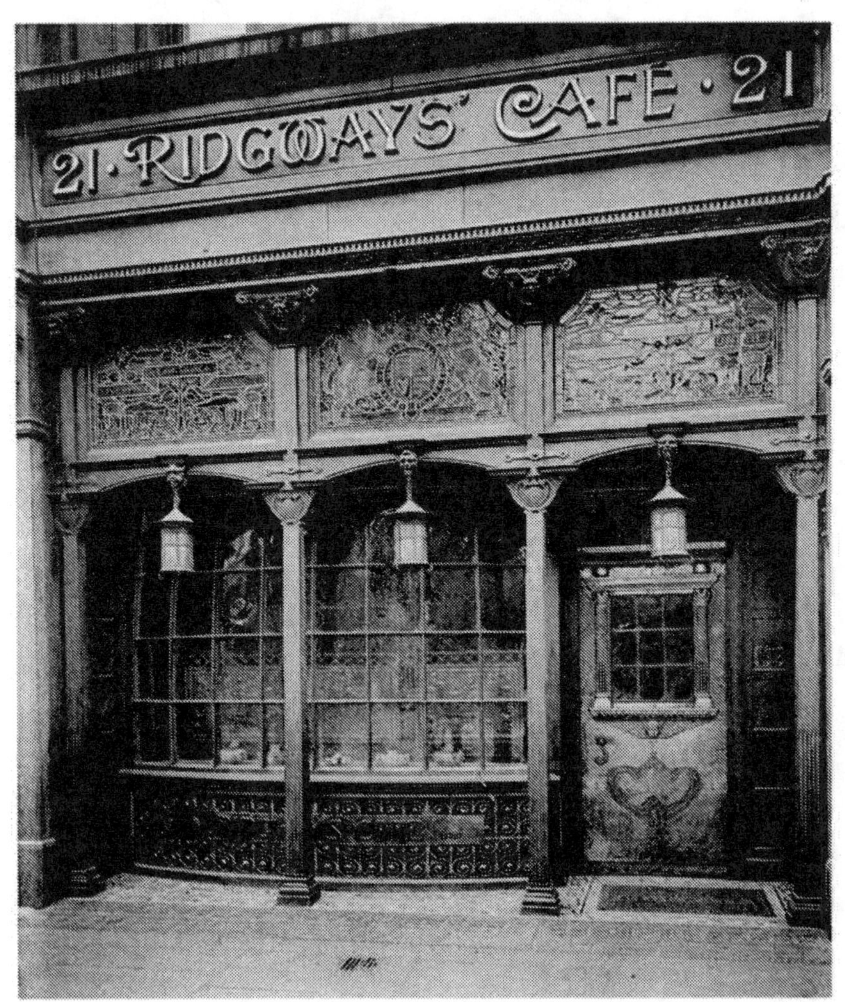

ST. ANNE'S STREET, MANCHESTER.

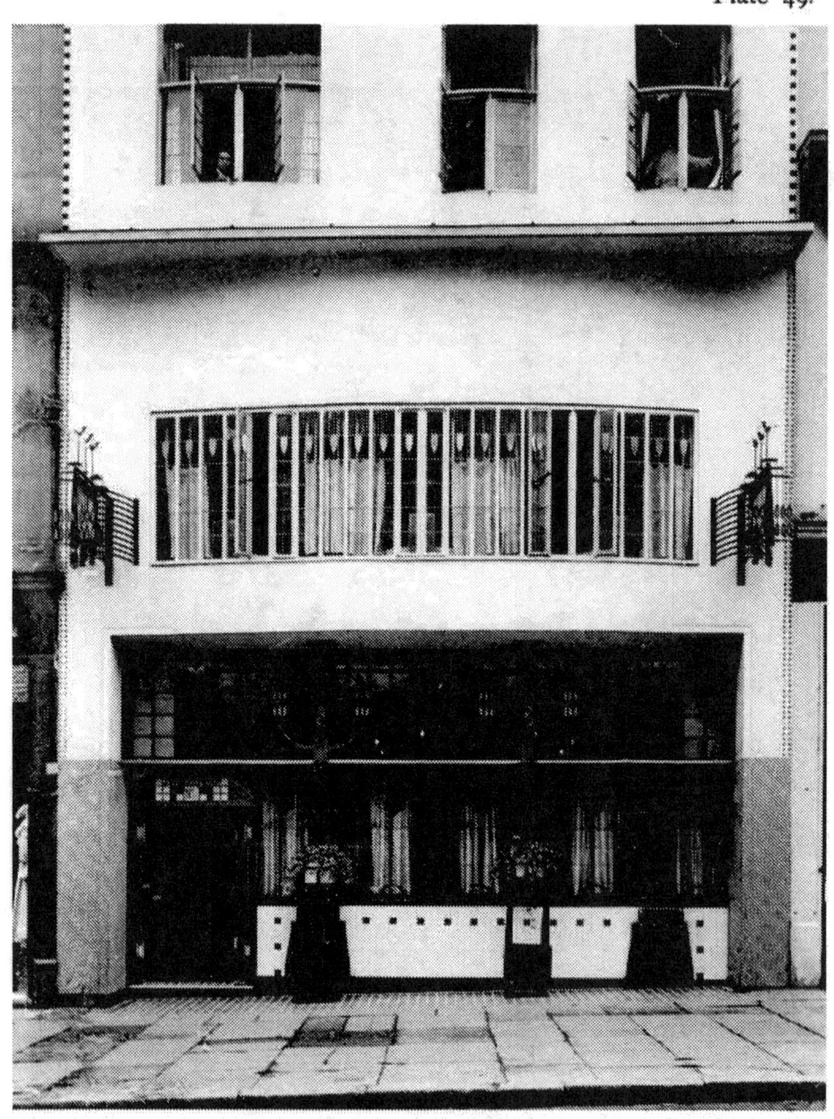

NO. 217, SAUCHIEHALL STREET, GLASGOW.

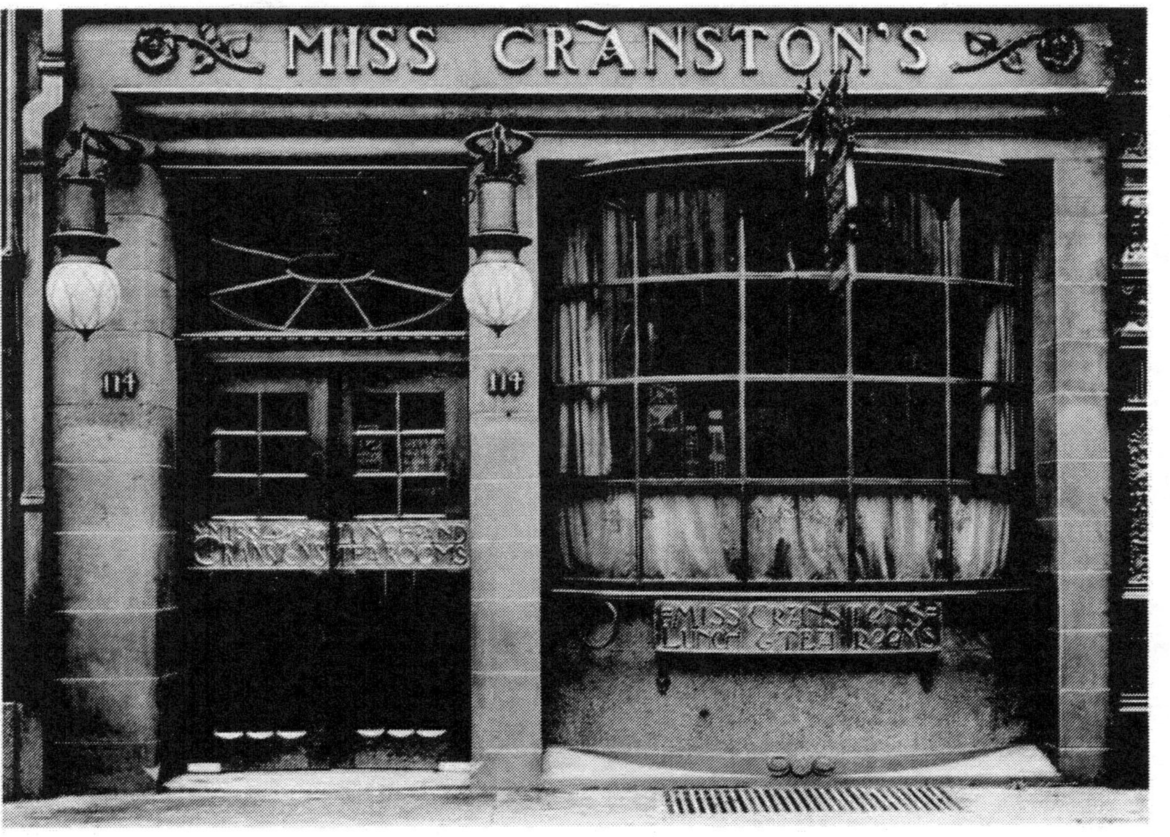

ARGYLL STREET, GLASGOW.

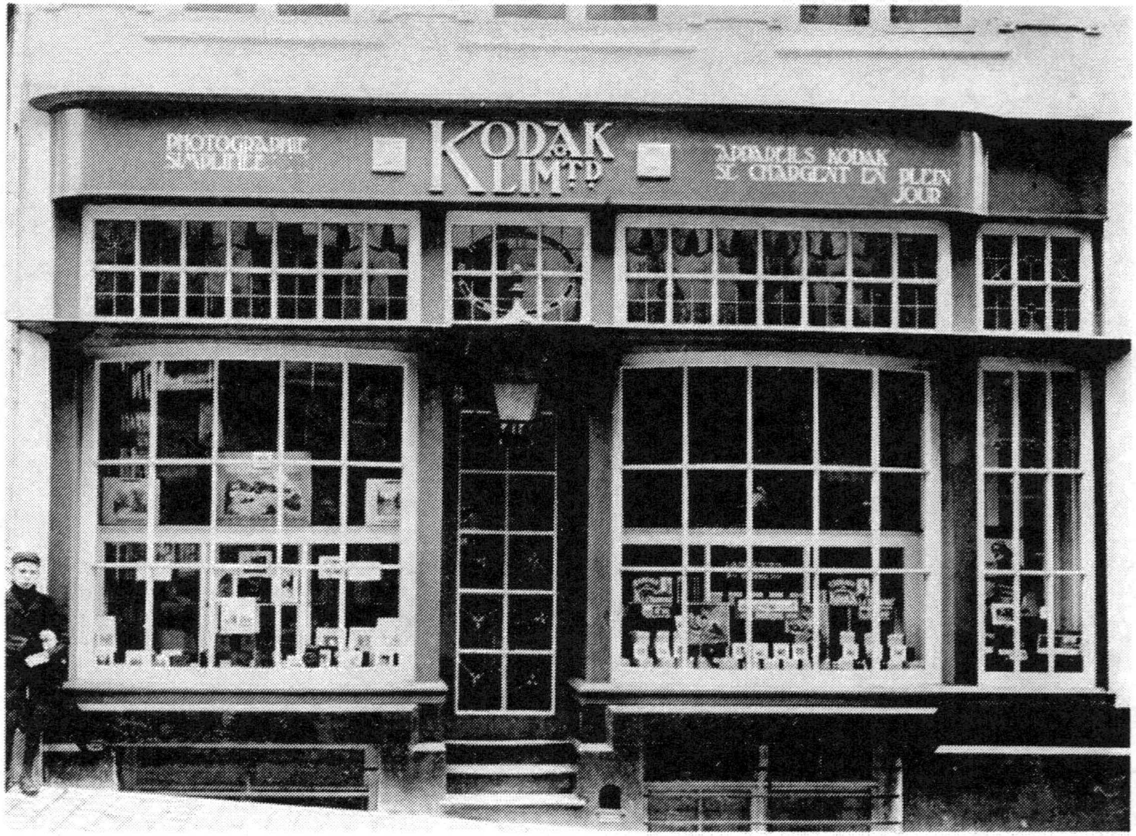

Plate 51.

MONTAGNE DE LA COUR, BRUSSELS.

Plate 52.

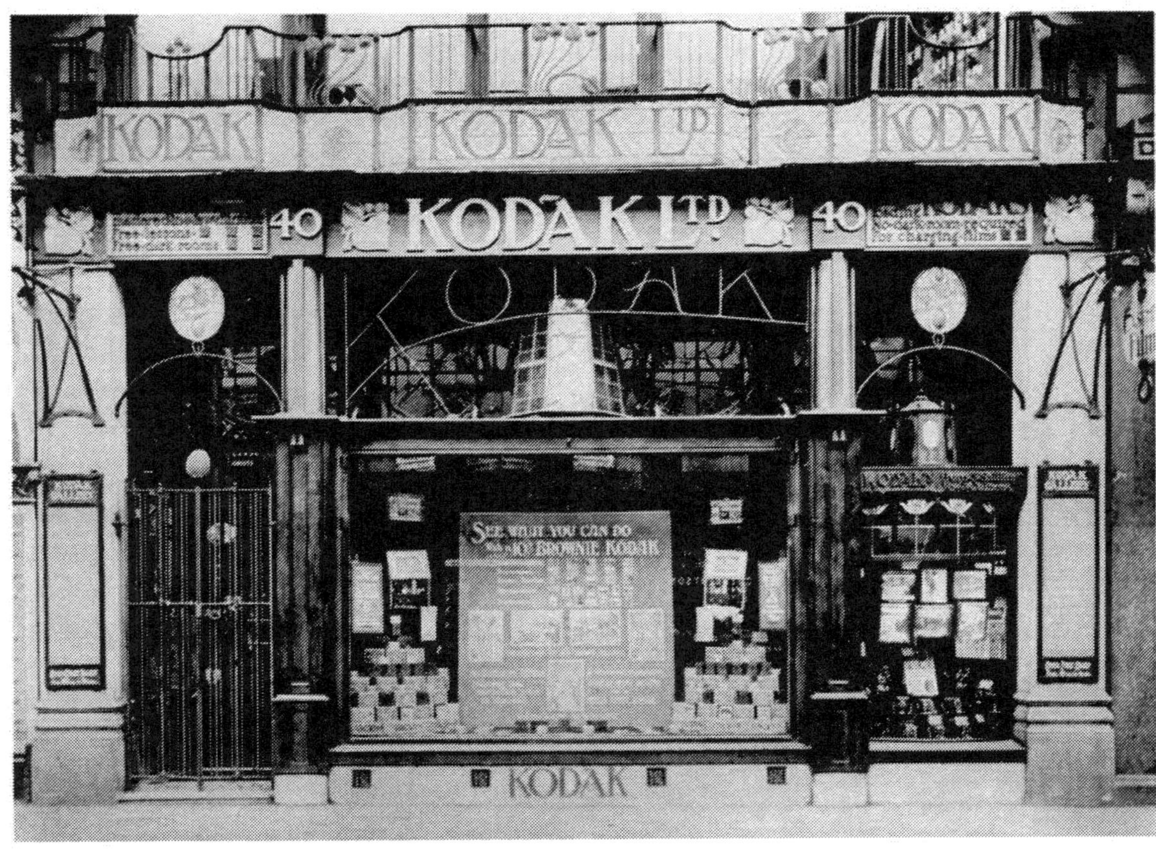

NO 40, WEST STRAND, LONDON.

www.ingramcontent.com/pod-product-compliance
Lightning Source LLC
LaVergne TN
LVHW080311110826
845155LV00023B/114

* 9 7 8 1 9 0 5 2 1 7 7 4 8 *